The FLYING BISCUIT Cafe
Cookbook

APRIL MOON

Illustrations by Wendy Weiner

LONGSTREET
Atlanta, Georgia

Published by LONGSTREET PRESS, INC.,
2974 Hardman Ct.
Atlanta, Georgia 30305

Printed in the United States of America

4th printing, 2002

Library of Congress Catalog Number 97-76259

ISBN: 1-56352-465-1

Cover and book design by Burtch Bennett Hunter
Typesetting by Jill Dible

TABLE OF CONTENTS

FOREWORD

One time, when April and I were first dating, she invited me over to her place for a light dinner. "I'll just throw a salad together," she said. To me (at least at that time), that meant some iceberg lettuce (probably two weeks old, growing gray hair) and a bottle of Italian dressing. Instead, April's thrown-together salad consisted of beautiful greens, two kinds of peppers, carrots, pine nuts, and sliced roast duck. Oh yes, she had chilled a bottle of champagne, too. A few months later, I was heating some canned tomato soup for us. "Is that all you're going to do?" she asked. "I thought I'd stir it, too," I replied. She immediately got out some oregano, thyme, Tabasco, and Worcestershire sauce and created some of the best tomato soup I have ever had.

Those examples sum up for me April's passion for food. Her love of food and its preparation is contagious, whether she is fixing something as simple as a can of soup or as complex as a four-course dinner. Happily for the rest of us, she loves to pass her joy and knowledge along: to those fortunate enough to work with her in the kitchen of the Flying Biscuit Cafe; to the students in her cooking classes; and now to our older daughter, Hana, who is finally showing an interest in food beyond boxed macaroni and cheese. In a few years, I imagine Hana's little sister, Emma, will begin her tutelage. Lucky you. You don't have to wait so long to enjoy this labor of love.

DAVID HARPER
Atlanta, Georgia

WHY A RESTAURANT?

After the birth of my first child, Hana, I decided to take a break from cooking for a while to be a full-time mommy. About six months later, funding for that position was running out. My first instinct was to look for something besides cooking to occupy my "spare time" (practically nonexistent with a six-month-old). About this time, opportunity came knocking at my door. Delia Champion, a former coworker from my previous restaurant gig, offered me a creative position developing a menu for a little dive of a spot she was planning to open in the Candler Park neighborhood of Atlanta. I took the job, eager for an opportunity to cook from my heart. The concept was to have a small restaurant that would serve sixty to seventy-five people a day. Much of the food would be vegetarian, a few items would be vegan, and some dishes would contain poultry and seafood. The concept would be upscale comfort food. We were going to serve breakfast all day, from eight-thirty in the morning until ten at night. The name of the restaurant was already decided—the Flying Biscuit Cafe.

One month later, we were serving 200 meals a day, and I was getting up at five in the morning to make biscuits.

Somehow, we lived through those first few months. As any restaurateur knows, you do whatever has to be done, and sooner or later the day will end. It is extremely hard work and extremely gratifying. Working in a restaurant is like performing a play live on stage. You get up there and create a dish, and when all your ingredients arrive on time and are fresh you have a good act. But you also count on the help and experience of the crew you work with to make the next act succeed. Executing certain dinner specials—for example, a dish like Roasted Poblano Pesto Pasta—requires special skill and finesse. The pasta can't be overcooked, the shrimp undercooked, or the sauce too spicy. Once the dinner has been plated, the final act commences. A wait person delivers the meal, and the rest of us on staff do whatever we can to make sure the customer is satisfied. When the patron is happy and nourished, that is applause to our ears. It is so fulfilling to watch someone enjoy a meal that you create, and that is why I work in a great restaurant, the Flying Biscuit Cafe.

WHY A COOKBOOK?

This cookbook is a tool. I wrote it for all those people who wanted the recipe for our Cranberry Apple Butter or our Flying Biscuits. There is really no trick or secret to any of these recipes, and nothing has been hidden. You may even find better ways to make some of these dishes. If you do, please write them down in this book. Make notes to yourself in the margins. If you like more garlic in the Balsamic Dressing, mark a change on the recipe. I want these recipes to be special to you, and by adding your own touches to the dishes, they will be. To me, the tattered edges of a cookbook are a sign that it contains some well-loved and cherished recipes.

JUST THE BASICS
On Equipment

All your pots and pans do not have to match in order for you to be a good cook. I recommend several heavy-bottomed saucepans and at least one high-quality nonstick pan for cooking the egg dishes in this book. A large, heavy-bottomed stockpot will also come in handy.

One high-quality eight-inch chef's knife, a good paring knife, and a serrated-edge knife will do just about all the chopping, dicing, slicing, and mincing you will need. Buy high-carbon steel knives, and do not run them through a dishwasher. Wash by hand as soon as you are finished using them and dry with a soft towel. High-quality knives do not have to be professionally sharpened as often as cheaper knives. Running the edge of the blade over a diamond steel at a forty-five degree angle will adequately sharpen the edge and lengthen the life of your knives. I prefer a plastic cutting board to a wooden one because it can be cleaned in the dishwasher.

Pot holders and cooling racks are indispensable.

A good instant-read thermometer helps make sure that meats are properly cooked. Poultry should always be cooked to 180°F.

Measuring spoons, measuring cups, wooden spoons, and rubber spatulas are a must. That old-fashioned potato masher will come in handy.

On Ingredients

I always tell people, be flexible. Our motto at the Biscuit is "we have everything, we just don't have everything all the time." Ingredients are often seasonal and regional. Georgia is known for Vidalia onions, but they may never appear in your locale. You may see Texas Sweet or Maui onions, so use those instead. You may never see good smoked salmon where you live, but if you can get smoked trout, use it. Utilize the freshest products you can obtain. The quality of these products will enhance any dish you are preparing.

Eggs — Use the freshest eggs you can find. The fresher the egg, the less likely it will break when you go to make that over-easy. Cartons are usually dated. One indication of an egg's freshness is how bright the yolk is. The fresher the egg the brighter the yolk. Always use large eggs when baking.

Butter — I always use unsalted butter. Food should be salted to taste, not by using salted butter. European-style butters such as Plugra are best because they are churned with little or no water added to them. Such butter creates tender baked goods and smooth butter sauces that will not separate.

Sugar — When a recipe in this book calls for just sugar, use granulated and measure it in dry measuring cups. Some recipes call for raw sugar (also called turbinado sugar). This is simply a coarsely ground unbleached sugar that has a slight molasses-like flavor. Other recipes will call for brown sugar. Always measure brown sugar by lightly packing it into a liquid measuring cup.

Flour — Most of my recipes calling for flour will say all-purpose flour, but there are exceptions. Recipes for tender baked goods, such as cookies, pie crusts, and biscuits, will call for soft winter wheat flour. This soft flour has less gluten than all-purpose flour and creates a more crumbly texture. Recipes for chewier baked goods, such as bread, will specify bread flour, which gives the baked item a firmer consistency.

Salt — I think that kosher salt has much more flavor than regular table salt, and I prefer to use it when cooking. The major exception to this is in baking. You will notice that recipes for baked goods call for just salt. Iodized salt has a finer ground and dissolves quicker than kosher salt, so there is less risk of salty pockets in muffins or cakes.

Oils — When I am sautéing I prefer to use canola oil or regular olive oil. They are light in taste and do not overpower the other ingredients in a dish. For times when I want more piquancy, such as when making pesto or dipping bread in oil, I like to use extra-virgin olive oil. Toasted nut oils such as sesame and walnut are always added at the end of the cooking process, because heat reduces the intensity of their flavor.

Herbs and Spices — Dried herbs and spices should be stored in a cool, dry place. Their aromatic qualities deteriorate when exposed to light and heat. Do not use them if they are more than a year old; they will have lost their essential flavors. Always use fresh herbs when called for. They have characteristics that are quite distinct from dried herbs, and also add color to dishes.

Peppers — At the Biscuit we use a wide variety of hot peppers. I have learned from experience that the spiciness is variable, and that a change of seasons brings a change in the intensity of a pepper's heat. Always add hot peppers gradually to whatever you are preparing, and taste as you go. Remember that the heat will increase the longer a dish sits with those tiny, fiery tidbits in it.

Pasta — Fresh pasta is not always available, but high-quality dried pasta can be acquired fairly easily at most groceries. Look for pasta that is made with 100 percent semolina flour. Cook pasta in plenty of salted water, but do not overcook. It should be *al dente* (firm to the tooth).

Seafood — Let your nose be your guide to purchasing fresh seafood. Delicious seafood should smell like the ocean, not fishy. The best way to buy fish is whole. To test for freshness, look for bright red gills and uncloudy eyes.

Poultry — Free-range chicken truly is the best. It has more flavor and less fat than conventionally raised chicken. Whenever it is available, I highly recommend using it.

One last thing. Everything can be made lower in fat. Butter can be substituted with prune puree in baking, cream can be changed to milk, and sour cream can be replaced with plain, nonfat yogurt. But remember, these changes will alter the ultimate quality of what you are preparing. I believe that moderation—not the elimination of all fat—is best. After all, fat adds flavor.

    The recipes that follow are what I feel make the Biscuit special. I hope that when you make them, you will feel as if you were sitting at a table in our little restaurant.

ACKNOWLEDGMENTS

Thanks to my parents, who always encouraged me to do what I really love: cook. To everyone who has shared some of their knowledge and inspiration with me—particularly Augie, Marianne, Merrijoy, and Alix—I am so grateful. Thank you Delia, for allowing me to share in your dream, the Flying Biscuit Cafe, and to Missy and Emily for believing in the dream and making it a reality. Thanks to Wendy Weiner for giving this book the look and feel of the Biscuit with her beautiful illustrations. Longstreet Press, I appreciate the opportunity you have given me to express myself and live my dream to write a cookbook. Suzanne De Galan, thank you for taking my jumble of words and creating a cohesive piece of work. I dedicate this book to David, Hana, and Emma, who always keep the home fires burning, because there is nothing more important than a big hug at the end of a hard day. Lastly, this book exists because of the endurance, loyalty, and hard work of all the people who have worked at the Flying Biscuit Cafe and given a little piece of themselves to this restaurant.

The FLYING BISCUIT Cafe Cookbook

Egg-Ceptional Egg Dishes

A farm-fresh egg is a beautiful thing to behold, a golden yellow sphere set against a glistening white backdrop. Eggs can say good morning at dawn or be a quick and light late-night dinner. Packed full of protein, these little gems satisfy many dietary requirements and can be prepared on the spur of the moment.

There are a few things to know in order to create the perfect egg dish. First, a good nonstick pan is indispensable. It will enable you to easily flip an over-easy egg or an omelet. (To obtain that professional technique, practice flipping dry beans in a dry sauté pan.) Second, do not cook an egg over high heat. The egg will become tough and rubbery. Low heat and patience will create tender, moist, and delicious results. Third, salting eggs before cooking will toughen them. Keep that salt on the table. And last, a cold egg is not very appetizing. Make the coffee and biscuits before you begin cooking the eggs. Serve these dishes straight out of the pan with a hot cup of joe and enjoy.

SMOKED SALMON SCRAMBLE

Since there are few ingredients in this dish, it is important to use only the best. There are several different grades of smoked salmon. Look for salmon with a reddish pink—not fuchsia—color. Fresh dill is easy to find at most grocery stores and grows like a weed in a sunny garden spot.

4 ounces smoked salmon
8 large eggs
4 ounces cream cheese, at room temperature
2 tablespoons chopped fresh dill
2 tablespoons unsalted butter
Freshly ground white pepper to taste

1. Break up salmon into bite-sized pieces.
2. In a medium bowl whisk eggs until light and frothy.
3. In a small bowl mash cream cheese and dill together with a wooden spoon.
4. In a large, nonstick sauté pan over medium heat, melt butter. Add eggs. While eggs are still soft and wet, stir in smoked salmon, cream cheese, and a grating of white pepper.
5. Using a rubber spatula, pull the eggs that are cooked on the edges of the pan to the center and gently shake the pan to redistribute the scramble evenly over the cooking surface. Continue to cook, moving the eggs from the side to the center of the pan every few minutes, until eggs reach desired consistency. Serve up hot.

Serves 6 to 8 people

VEGGIE SCRAMBLE

Don't confine yourself to the squash and peppers in this recipe. Use what is seasonal and locally available.

8 large eggs
1 small zucchini
1 small yellow squash
1 small yellow onion
1 small red bell pepper
1 small green bell pepper
1 tablespoon unsalted butter
½ cup grated mozzarella cheese

1. In a medium bowl whisk eggs until light and frothy.
2. Quarter the zucchini and squash lengthwise, then cut them diagonally into ½-inch pieces. Cut onion, red pepper, and green pepper lengthwise into ¼-inch slices.
3. In a large, nonstick sauté pan over medium heat, melt butter. Add the cut vegetables. Cook until the squash is tender and the onions are just beginning to turn translucent.
4. Add the eggs to the sauté pan and continue to cook over medium heat. While eggs are still wet in the center but beginning to cook on the edges of the pan, add the grated mozzarella.
5. Using a rubber spatula, pull the eggs that are cooked on the edges of the pan to the center and gently shake the pan to redistribute the scramble evenly over the cooking surface. Continue to cook, moving the eggs from the side to the center of the pan every few minutes, until eggs reach desired consistency.

Serves 6 to 8 people

BRIE AND ASPARAGUS SCRAMBLE

This is a great spring brunch dish.

8 large eggs
½ pound asparagus
1 tablespoon unsalted butter
6 ounces ripe Brie, cut into 1-inch pieces
1 tablespoon minced fresh tarragon

1. In a medium bowl whisk eggs until light and frothy.
2. Remove the tough bottom ends of the asparagus and discard. Cut the remaining asparagus on the diagonal into 1-inch pieces. Cook asparagus in a small pot of boiling water until it is just tender and turns bright green. Remove from water and rinse under cold water to stop the cooking process.
3. In a large, nonstick sauté pan over medium heat, melt butter. Add eggs and asparagus. Once eggs are beginning to cook on the edges of the pan but still wet in the center, add Brie.
4. Using a rubber spatula, pull the eggs that are cooked on the edges of the pan to the center and gently shake the pan to redistribute the scramble evenly over the cooking surface. Continue to cook over medium heat, moving the eggs from the side to the center of the pan every few minutes, until eggs reach desired consistency. Heap the scramble onto plates and sprinkle with tarragon.

Serves 6 to 8 people

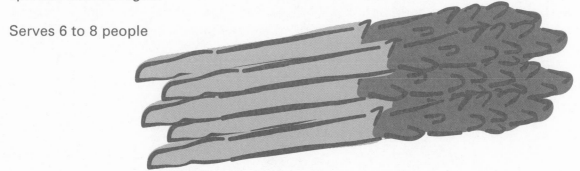

NOODLES AND EGGS

This recipe was introduced to me long before the Biscuit by my good friend Lynne Sawicki. She said it was a specialty of her mother's when she was growing up. She also claimed it was a great cure for a bad hangover. This is a good way to use up leftover cooked pasta.

6 large eggs
2 cups fresh spinach, washed
½ pound button mushrooms
1 small onion
1 tablespoon unsalted butter
½ pound penne pasta or other leftover pasta,
  cooked, drained, and cooled
½ cup ricotta cheese
2 teaspoons Moon Dust (recipe on page 40)

1. In a medium bowl whisk eggs until light and frothy.
2. Prepare the vegetables. Roughly chop cleaned spinach. Slice button mushrooms into ¼-inch slices. Peel onion and slice into ¼-inch rings.
3. In a large, nonstick sauté pan over medium-high heat, melt butter. Add pasta. Stir pasta frequently until it begins to brown, then add the prepared vegetables. Cook until onions begin to turn translucent. Add eggs to the pan. Once the eggs begin to cook on the edges of the pan, move them to the center and stir in the ricotta cheese. When eggs reach desired consistency, remove from heat, season with Moon Dust, and serve.

Serves 6 to 8 people

MEGGXICAN WRAP

This dish and Egg-Ceptional Eggs, Biscuit Style, are two of the most popular egg dishes at the restaurant. Warm the Red Salsa before topping the tortilla so the scramble inside stays nice and hot.

8 large eggs
1 small tomato
1 small yellow onion
1 serrano pepper
1 tablespoon unsalted butter
½ cup grated sharp cheddar cheese
4 8-inch flour tortillas

GARNISHES
1 cup Red Salsa (recipe on page 98)
½ cup sour cream

1. In a medium bowl whisk eggs until light and frothy.
2. Prepare the vegetables. Core tomato and dice into ½-inch pieces. Peel onion, cut in half lengthwise, and slice lengthwise into ¼-inch pieces. Mince the serrano pepper. If you prefer less heat, remove the seeds.
3. In a large, nonstick sauté pan over medium heat, melt butter. Add the onion and serrano. Cook until onions begin to turn translucent.
4. Add eggs. When the eggs begin to cook on the edges of the pan, pull them to the center and shake the pan gently to redistribute the scramble. While the eggs are still soft, add the tomato and grated cheddar. Continue to cook until eggs reach desired consistency. As the eggs are finishing, drape the tortillas over the eggs in the hot pan to warm and soften them.
5. Place one tortilla on each person's plate. Fill with the hot scrambled eggs, fold the tortilla in half, and top with Red Salsa and a dollop of sour cream.

Serves 4 people

SUN-DRIED TOMATO OMELET

This recipe is for one huge six-egg omelet. People eat these by themselves all the time at the restaurant, but I think after you read the recipe, you might prefer to share it. Use good quality sun-dried tomatoes packed in oil. To perfect your omelet-flipping technique, practice with dried beans in a cold sauté pan.

6 large eggs
4 to 5 sun-dried tomatoes in olive oil, drained
5 to 6 fresh basil leaves
1 tablespoon unsalted butter
¼ cup ricotta cheese
¼ cup grated mozzarella cheese

1. In a medium bowl whisk eggs until light and frothy.
2. Cut sun-dried tomatoes into ¼-inch pieces. Coarsely chop basil.
3. In medium nonstick sauté pan over moderate heat, melt butter. When butter bubbles, add eggs.
4. Cook over medium heat until eggs begin to set on the edges of the sauté pan. With a rubber spatula, pull the eggs from the edges of the pan to the center and shake the pan gently to redistribute the eggs evenly over the cooking surface. Continue this motion until the eggs are cooked on the bottom of the pan but still wet on top. With a quick jerking motion, pull the pan toward you to flip the omelet. Fill with ricotta cheese, grated mozzarella, sun-dried tomatoes, and chopped basil. Gently turn omelet onto a serving plate and flip in half to make a semicircle.

Serves 1 very hungry or 2 moderately hungry people

GREEK SCRAMBLE WITH ARTICHOKES, BLACK OLIVES, AND FETA

This is a scramble with a Mediterranean flair.

8 large eggs
1 (15 ounce) can of artichokes, drained
½ cup ricotta cheese
½ cup grated mozzarella cheese
¼ cup grated Asiago cheese
¼ teaspoon ground nutmeg
½ teaspoon black pepper
6 to 8 fresh basil leaves
8 to 10 kalamata olives
1 tablespoon unsalted butter

GARNISH
2 tablespoons crumbled feta cheese

1. In a medium bowl whisk eggs until light and frothy.
2. Quarter artichokes. Place in a medium bowl with ricotta, mozzarella, Asiago, nutmeg, and pepper. Coarsely chop basil and add to bowl. Gently combine all ingredients in bowl with a wooden spoon and set aside.
3. Remove pits from olives, then coarsely chop.
4. In a large, nonstick sauté pan over medium heat, melt butter. When butter bubbles, add eggs. Cook over medium heat until eggs begin to set on the edges of the pan. With a rubber spatula, pull eggs at the edges of the pan to the center and gently shake the pan to redistribute the scramble. Continue this motion every few minutes until eggs are almost done but still wet. Add the cheese mixture in heaping tablespoons over the top of scramble. Stir in cheeses to combine and sprinkle with olives. Remove from heat and garnish with crumbled feta cheese.

Serves 6 to 8 people

EGG-CEPTIONAL EGGS, BISCUIT STYLE

This and the Flying Biscuit Breakfast (consisting of eggs, potatoes, and turkey sausage) are the two most popular items on our brunch menu. On Sundays alone we serve seventy-five to eighty portions of this with heaping sides of potatoes. Even though this is a lot, it works out okay because the kitchen can execute Egg-Ceptional Eggs fairly quickly by preparing the Love Cakes ahead of time and then cooking up the eggs and sautéing the Love Cakes to order. Topped with Green Salsa, these eggs truly are an exceptional dish.

2 teaspoons unsalted butter
2 large eggs
2 teaspoons canola oil
2 Love Cakes (recipe on page 22)

GARNISHES
2 tablespoons Green Salsa (recipe on page 99)
1 tablespoon sour cream
1 tablespoon crumbled feta cheese
2 to 3 very thin slices of red onion

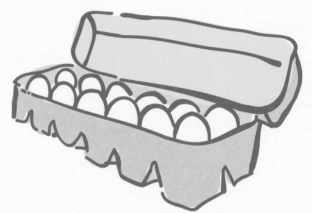

1. In a small nonstick sauté pan over medium heat, melt butter. Gently crack eggs into pan so that the yolks do not break. In a second small sauté pan over medium-high heat, heat canola oil. Lightly brown Love Cakes on both sides.
2. When the whites of the eggs are almost fully cooked, flip the eggs over and cook to desired consistency. Place Love Cakes on a serving plate and top with eggs. Garnish with Green Salsa, sour cream, feta, and red onion.

Serves 1

Sweet Starts

I remember how special it was to have pancakes or French toast for dinner when I was a child. Sweet stacks of thirsty cakes soaking up real maple syrup were always a treat. At the Biscuit we make gallons of pancake batter from scratch to serve for our weekend brunches. We try to serve our pancakes with a seasonal flair, offering Sweet Potato Pancakes in the fall and Ricotta Pancakes with Very Berry Compote in the summer. Our French toast is made with the bread we bake fresh daily in the bakery, and it eagerly absorbs the eggy custard before being browned on the griddle. By the way, I highly recommend a griddle for those pancake and French toast fans out there. It will enable you to cook more cakes at a time, and it will cook them more evenly than a sauté pan. But if you don't have a griddle, a frying pan will do. Don't let that stand in the way of having a sweet start to your day.

HEARTY ORGANIC OATMEAL PANCAKES

The secret to these hearty pancakes is patience. The oats must soak at least two hours, and the cakes should cook over medium-low heat. If the heat is too high, the cakes will brown on the outside but still be raw in the center. Use regular rolled oats, not the quick-cook variety; the texture of the oats is what makes these pancakes so good. A liberal slathering of butter and maple syrup makes this a very fulfilling breakfast.

2 cups organic rolled oats
2 cups nonfat buttermilk
2 large eggs, lightly beaten
4 tablespoons unsalted butter, melted and cooled
½ cup all-purpose flour
2 tablespoons sugar
1 teaspoon baking powder
1 teaspoon baking soda
½ teaspoon ground cinnamon
¼ teaspoon salt
Canola oil for griddle

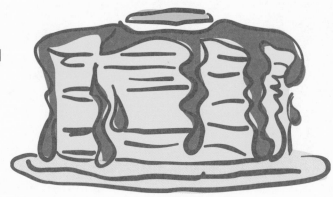

TOPPINGS
Butter
Warm maple syrup

1. Combine oats and buttermilk in a large bowl. Cover and refrigerate for 2 hours, or overnight.
2. Add eggs and melted butter to oat mixture.
3. Sift together flour, sugar, baking powder, baking soda, cinnamon, and salt. Add to oat mixture.
4. Preheat griddle over medium-low heat and lightly coat with canola oil. Ladle batter in ¼-cup measurements onto griddle. Spread out batter with the back of the ladle. When bubbles appear, gently flip cakes and cook until golden brown, about 5 minutes per side. Serve hot.

Makes about 20 pancakes, serving 6 to 8 people

RICOTTA PANCAKES

These cakes are almost the opposite of the Hearty Organic Oatmeal Pancakes. They are light and fluffy in texture—and cook up quickly.

2 cups all-purpose flour
2 teaspoons baking powder
1 teaspoon baking soda
½ teaspoon salt
2 tablespoons sugar
6 tablespoons unsalted butter, melted and cooled
1 cup ricotta cheese
1 ½ cups milk
1 large egg
¼ teaspoon vanilla extract
Pinch of nutmeg
Canola oil for griddle

TOPPINGS
Maple syrup
Fresh Berry Compote (recipe on page 111)

1. In a large bowl sift together flour, baking powder, baking soda, salt, and sugar.
2. In a medium bowl whisk together melted butter, ricotta, milk, egg, vanilla, and nutmeg.
3. Make a well in the center of the dry ingredients and pour in the ricotta mixture. Stir together with a wooden spoon until just combined. Batter should look lumpy. Do not overmix.
4. Place a griddle or large sauté pan over medium-high heat. Lightly coat with canola oil and ladle ¼ cup batter onto griddle for each cake. When bubbles appear, gently flip the cakes and cook until lightly browned. Serve hot off the griddle, with warm maple syrup or Fresh Berry Compote.

Makes about 18 cakes, serving 5 to 6 people

SOUR CREAM BANANA PANCAKES

These cakes remind me of banana bread fresh from the oven. Children seem to love them. If you wish to capture that childhood comfort feeling, sprinkle some chocolate chips into the batter before you ladle them onto the griddle. I like to top these with honey and sautéed bananas sometimes, but warm maple syrup does great in a pinch.

2 cups all-purpose flour
1 tablespoon plus ½ teaspoon baking powder
2 teaspoons baking soda
¼ cup sugar
¾ teaspoon salt
¼ teaspoon ground nutmeg
2 cups ripe, mashed bananas (about 4 bananas)
2 large eggs
½ cup sour cream
½ cup milk
¾ teaspoon vanilla extract
6 tablespoons unsalted butter, melted and cooled
Canola oil for griddle

TOPPINGS
Honey
Sautéed bananas
Maple syrup

1. Sift flour, baking powder, baking soda, sugar, salt, and nutmeg into a large mixing bowl.
2. In a medium mixing bowl whisk together bananas, eggs, sour cream, milk, vanilla, and butter.
3. Make a well in the center of the dry ingredients and add the banana mixture. Using a wooden spoon, gently combine until liquids are just incorporated into the dry ingredients. Do not overmix.
4. Place a griddle or large sauté pan over medium-high heat. Lightly coat with canola oil and ladle batter onto hot griddle with a ¼-cup measure. As bubbles appear on the top of batter, gently flip cakes over and cook until lightly brown on both sides. Serve hot, with honey and sautéed bananas or warm maple syrup.

Makes about 18 to 20 cakes, serving 5 to 6 people

SWEET POTATO PANCAKES

These cakes are a great way to utilize leftover sweet potatoes. It you are not using leftover sweets, place two small sweet potatoes in a pot of water and cook until tender. Run cold water over the hot potatoes until cool enough to handle, then slip off the skin and mash.

2 cups all-purpose flour
2 tablespoons sugar
2 teaspoons baking powder
½ teaspoon salt
1 teaspoon ground cinnamon
¼ teaspoon ground nutmeg
1 ½ cups milk
1 cup cooked, peeled, and mashed sweet potatoes
2 large eggs
8 tablespoons (1 stick) unsalted butter, melted and cooled
½ teaspoon vanilla extract
Canola oil for griddle

TOPPINGS
Butter
Warm maple syrup

1. In a large bowl sift together flour, sugar, baking powder, salt, cinnamon, and nutmeg.
2. In a second large bowl whisk together milk, sweet potatoes, eggs, butter, and vanilla. Make a well in the center of the dry ingredients and add the sweet potato mixture. Stir together gently with a wooden spoon until ingredients are just combined. Do not overmix.
3. Place a griddle or large sauté pan over medium-high heat and lightly coat with canola oil. Ladle batter onto hot griddle in ¼-cup measurements and cook until bubbles appear on the surface of the cakes. Gently flip and cook until light brown. Serve with butter and warm maple syrup.

Makes about 18 to 20 cakes, serving 5 to 6 people

CUSTARD PANCAKE

This is not like the other pancakes included in this book. Instead, it is similar to those colossal Dutch pancakes. At the Biscuit there is not enough oven space to finish this pancake off in the oven (this oven cooking is what gives the pancake that final growth burst), so instead we cook it like an omelet, which gives it a dense, custardy consistency.

½ cup all-purpose flour
2 tablespoons sugar
¼ teaspoon salt
½ teaspoon almond extract

½ cup milk
3 large eggs
1 tablespoon unsalted butter
1 tablespoon sugar for sautéing

TOPPINGS
½ cup fresh seasonal fruit, such as blueberries,
  raspberries, or sliced peaches
¼ cup vanilla yogurt
1 tablespoon confectioners' sugar

1. Whisk together flour, 2 tablespoons of sugar, salt, almond extract, milk, and eggs in mixing bowl. Batter will appear lumpy, but do not worry. Cover and chill mixture for at least 1 hour before proceeding.
2. Place a large nonstick sauté pan over medium-high heat. Add ½ tablespoon of butter to the pan. When butter is bubbly, add pancake batter. Cook until mixture begins to set around the edges of the pan. Using a rubber spatula, move the batter from the edges to the center of the pan and gently shake to redistribute the mixture. Continue doing this until pancake is almost totally cooked.
3. Invert pancake onto a plate and add the remaining ½ tablespoon butter to the sauté pan. Sprinkle in 1 tablespoon of sugar and slide pancake back into the sauté pan to lightly brown the other side. Once cooked, turn out pancake onto a serving plate and top with fruit and yogurt. Sprinkle with confectioners' sugar.

Serves 2 to 3 people

GINGER CRAISIN PANCAKES

These cakes are similar to gingerbread in flavor. Craisins, which are dried, sweetened cranberries, add a nice tart contrast to the spices. They are becoming fairly easy to find, but you can substitute raisins if craisins are unavailable.

½ cup craisins
3 tablespoons sugar
1 cup all-purpose flour
½ cup graham cracker crumbs
⅛ teaspoon salt
1 tablespoon plus 2 teaspoons baking powder
¼ teaspoon ground cinnamon
¼ teaspoon ground cloves

¼ teaspoon ground nutmeg
2 teaspoons ground ginger
3 large eggs
1 ⅔ cups milk
3 ½ tablespoons unsalted butter, melted and cooled
1 tablespoon plus 2 teaspoons molasses
Canola oil for griddle

1. Place craisins, sugar, flour, graham cracker crumbs, salt, baking powder, and spices in a large mixing bowl. Stir with a wooden spoon to combine.
2. In a second large bowl combine eggs, milk, butter, and molasses and whisk together to break eggs and combine ingredients. Make a well in the center of the dry ingredients and add the egg-milk mixture. Stir with a wooden spoon until just mixed.
3. Place a large sauté pan or griddle over medium-high heat. Lightly coat with canola oil. Using a ¼-cup measure, ladle batter onto griddle. When bubbles appear on the surface of the cakes, gently flip and cook until golden brown. Serve hot off the griddle, with warm maple syrup or blackstrap molasses.

Makes 18 to 20 cakes, serving 4 to 5 people

ORANGE FRENCH TOAST

A few items on the Biscuit menu are considered staples. Orange French Toast is one of these. Lighter than regular French toast because it contains no cream or milk, and made with our Mushy Whole-Wheat Bread, this recipe lives up to our healthy standards. Topped with caramelized bananas, the recipe fulfills our taste standards as well.

CARAMELIZED BANANAS
2 to 3 firm but ripe bananas
2 tablespoons unsalted butter
2 tablespoons light brown sugar
2 tablespoons honey

BATTER
¼ cup sugar
⅛ teaspoon salt
1 ½ teaspoons vanilla extract
2 cups fresh orange juice
Grated zest of 1 orange

3 large eggs
Canola oil for griddle
2 loaves Mushy Whole-Wheat
Bread (recipe on page 68),
    cut into 1-inch-thick slices

1. To caramelize the bananas, peel the bananas and slice them on the diagonal into ½-inch slices. Place a medium nonstick sauté pan over medium-high heat and melt butter. Add the sliced bananas. Sprinkle brown sugar and honey over the top of the bananas and cook until the fruit begins to brown and the sugar is dissolved into the honey. Keep caramelized bananas warm while you make the French toast.

2. In a large bowl combine sugar, salt, vanilla, orange juice, orange zest, and eggs. Whisk all ingredients together until light and frothy.

3. Place a large sauté pan or griddle over medium-high heat and lightly coat with canola oil. Dip the slices of bread into the batter, then place them on the preheated griddle. Cook toast until light brown on both sides. Remove to a platter or individual plates. Carefully pour the caramelized bananas over the top of the French toast and serve with additional honey or maple syrup.

Makes about 16 to 20 pieces, serving 6 to 8 people

BUTTERMILK FRENCH TOAST

This low-fat French toast has a unique, tangy flavor from the buttermilk. We like to make this with Sour Cream Potato Bread and top it with Fresh Berry Compote.

4 large eggs
1 cup nonfat buttermilk
¼ teaspoon vanilla extract
¼ teaspoon ground cinnamon
Pinch of ground nutmeg
Pinch of salt
¼ cup sugar
Canola oil for griddle
1 loaf of Sour Cream Potato Bread (recipe on page 67), cut into 1-inch-thick slices

TOPPING
Fresh Berry Compote (recipe on page 111)

1. Crack eggs into a large mixing bowl and add buttermilk, vanilla, cinnamon, nutmeg, salt, and sugar. Whisk with a wire whip until well combined.
2. Place a griddle or large sauté pan over medium-high heat. Brush canola oil over the griddle surface. Dip slices of bread into the batter. Place on griddle and cook until lightly browned on both sides. Serve topped with Fresh Berry Compote.

Makes 8 to 10 slices, serving 4 to 5 people

STUFFED FRENCH TOAST

This French toast takes a little more time than the average French toast recipe, but the results are worth the extra effort. You can assemble the French toast the night before and cook it the next morning. Serve the slices cut in half on a puddle of fresh Razzberry Sauce, and you will be adored for the rest of the day.

1 (4 ounce) package cream cheese, at room temperature
1 tablespoon sugar
¼ teaspoon vanilla extract
1 loaf Sour Cream Potato Bread (recipe on page 67),
  cut into ¾-inch-thick slices
¼ cup raspberry jam
Buttermilk French Toast batter (recipe on page 17)
1 ½ cups chopped pistachio nuts
Canola oil for griddle

TOPPINGS
Razzberry Sauce (recipe on page 112)
Maple syrup

1. In a small mixing bowl combine cream cheese, sugar, and vanilla. Mix until smooth.
2. Spread 2 tablespoons of cream cheese mixture over 1 slice of the bread. On a second slice of bread spread 1 tablespoon raspberry jam. Sandwich the two pieces together and continue until all the bread slices are used.
3. Dip the sandwiches in the Buttermilk French Toast batter and let excess batter drain off. Spread the pistachios on a plate, press the sandwiches into the pistachios, and let sit for at least 15 minutes. Or wrap the sandwiches in waxed paper and refrigerate overnight.
4. Place a griddle or large sauté pan over medium heat. Lightly coat with canola oil. Place the stuffed sandwiches on the hot griddle and cook until the nuts begin to brown. Flip and cook on the second side. Cut each sandwich in half diagonally and serve on a puddle of Razzberry Sauce or topped with warm maple syrup.

Makes 8 to 10 slices, serving 4 to 5 people

CRUNCHY GRANOLA

At the Biscuit we serve granola over the top of a bowl of organic low-fat vanilla yogurt, then top the whole thing with fresh fruit. Delicious, and so nutritious.

3 tablespoons dark brown sugar
3 tablespoons honey
1 ¼ teaspoons sesame oil
¾ teaspoon ground cinnamon
¼ teaspoon vanilla extract
¼ teaspoon almond extract
2 cups organic rolled oats
⅓ cup hulled sesame seeds
⅓ cup sliced blanched almonds
½ cup whole unblanched almonds
⅓ cup craisins (dried cranberries)
⅓ cup golden raisins

1. Preheat oven to 350°F.
2. Place brown sugar, honey, sesame oil, cinnamon, vanilla, and almond extract in a heavy-bottomed saucepan. Place over low heat, stir, and cook just until sugar is dissolved. Remove from heat and set aside.
3. Add rolled oats and sesame seeds to the saucepan, mix well, and spread mixture over a lightly oiled jelly roll pan. Bake for 10 minutes. Sprinkle sliced and whole almonds on mixture and bake an additional 5 minutes to toast the nuts. Remove from oven and cool.
4. Turn mixture into a bowl and mix in craisins and raisins. Stored in an airtight container, granola will keep at room temperature for 2 weeks.

Makes 4 ½ cups

Specialties of the House

The recipes that follow are tried and true at the Flying Biscuit. They have endured since we opened our doors, and they remain customer favorites. I think they have been so successful because they are comfort foods—not too complex in flavor and like old faithful companions. They are recipes made with love, because their origins are rooted deep in our family traditions and memories. I hope when you serve Turkey Meatloaf or Mac and Cheese, it will create a feel-good mood at your table.

TURKEY MEATLOAF

There are very few things more comforting than a slice of meatloaf and a pile of mashed potatoes. We sell more meatloaf on Sunday evenings than any other time during the week. I believe that people want to stoke up for the work week ahead. The leftovers make great sandwiches.

2 tablespoons canola oil
3 ribs celery, minced
½ large yellow onion, minced
2 small carrots, grated
3 garlic cloves, minced
1 ½ tablespoons dried basil
1 ½ tablespoons dried oregano
2 tablespoons chopped fresh rosemary
1 ½ teaspoons freshly ground black pepper

1 ½ teaspoons kosher salt
1 ⅔ cups bread crumbs
2 large eggs
¼ cup heavy cream
2 tablespoons sun-dried tomatoes in oil, minced
½ cup freshly grated Parmesan cheese
¾ cup shredded mozzarella cheese
½ cup ketchup
2 pounds lean ground turkey

GARNISH
Creamy Horseradish Sauce (recipe on page 101)

1. Preheat oven to 350°F. Line bottom and sides of two 8½ x 4½-inch loaf pans with waxed paper and set aside.
2. In a large skillet heat the canola oil over medium-high heat. Add celery, onion, carrots, and garlic to the pan and sauté until onions are translucent and carrots have softened, about 7 minutes. Add the basil, oregano, rosemary, pepper, and salt to the vegetables. Sauté briefly to bring out the flavor of the herbs. Remove from heat and cool.
3. In a large bowl combine the contents from the skillet with the bread crumbs, eggs, cream, sun-dried tomatoes, Parmesan, mozzarella, ketchup, and turkey. Mix by hand until all ingredients are incorporated, then mound mixture into prepared loaf pans.
4. Bake 1 hour, or until the internal temperature on an instant-read meat thermometer reaches 180°F. Cool slightly, then cut and serve topped with Creamy Horseradish Sauce.

Serves 6 to 10 people generously

LOVE CAKES

(Black Bean Cakes)

Love Cakes are a staple at the Biscuit. Masa de harina is a superfine cornmeal that acts as the binder for these cakes. It has no substitute, but it's easy to find in a Mexican market. Use sparingly, because too much masa can make the cakes dry and crumbly. One final note: As you are standing at your sauté pan cooking these little black cakes, let the love flow.

2 (15 ounce) cans cooked black beans
2 tablespoons canola oil
2 tablespoons minced yellow onion
2 garlic cloves, minced
1 teaspoon ground cumin
1 teaspoon kosher salt
¼ cup masa de harina

GARNISHES
½ cup Green Salsa (recipe on page 99)
2 tablespoons crumbled feta cheese
¼ cup slivered red onions

1. Rinse and drain black beans in a sieve.
2. In a small sauté pan heat 1 tablespoon of the canola oil over medium heat. Cook onion, garlic, cumin, and salt until onions are translucent.
3. Place drained beans and onion mixture in a bowl and mash with a potato masher until well combined. Gradually add masa, allowing mixture to absorb it before adding more. Test dough by rolling it in the palm of your hand. Keep adding masa until dough doesn't stick to your hand and holds the shape of a ball.
4. Divide dough into 16 small balls and flatten into cakes. Place a large skillet over medium heat and add the remaining 1 tablespoon of canola oil. Sauté cakes until lightly browned on each side, about 3 to 5 minutes per side. Top with Green Salsa, feta cheese, and slivered red onions.

Makes 16 cakes, serving 8 people

VIRTUOUS VEGAN PIE

We often serve this dish in a less-than-virtuous manner, topped with Jack cheese and sour cream. This recipe makes five single-serving pies.

1 tablespoon canola oil
½ teaspoon chili powder
½ teaspoon ground cumin
¼ teaspoon cayenne pepper
½ teaspoon kosher salt
¼ teaspoon freshly ground black pepper
2 small zucchini, cut into ½-inch dice
2 small yellow squash, cut into ½-inch dice
1 green bell pepper, seeded and cut into ½-inch dice
1 red bell pepper, seeded and cut into ½-inch dice
½ small onion, cut into ½-inch dice
15 six-inch corn tortillas
1 cup canola oil for blanching the corn tortillas

GARNISHES
Spiced Pumpkin Seeds
Jack cheese
Sour cream
Green Salsa (recipe on page 99)

SPICED PUMPKIN SEEDS
1 cup hulled raw pumpkin seeds
½ teaspoon cayenne pepper
½ teaspoon chili powder
2 teaspoons ground cumin
¼ teaspoon ground cinnamon
½ teaspoon kosher salt
½ teaspoon freshly ground black pepper
1 teaspoon canola oil

1. Preheat oven to 350°F. Heat 1 tablespoon of canola oil in a large sauté pan over medium-high heat. Sauté chili powder, cumin, cayenne, salt, and pepper with diced vegetables. Cook until vegetables just begin to feel tender. Remove vegetables from pan and place in a strainer to drain excess moisture. Set aside.
2. Prepare Spiced Pumpkin Seeds. In a medium bowl mix all pumpkin seed ingredients until seeds are well coated with spices. Turn seeds onto a small sheet pan and cook in preheated oven for 10 minutes. Cool and set aside.

3. Heat 1 cup of the canola oil in a medium sauté pan over medium-high heat. To test whether the oil is hot enough, dip the edge of a tortilla in it. It should sizzle. When oil is hot, dip corn tortillas in the oil for 3 to 5 seconds. (You want to soften the tortillas. If they become crisp, you have cooked them too long.) Drain on paper towels to remove excess oil.

4. Assemble the pies. Place 5 of the tortillas on a sheet pan, top each with drained veggies, and sprinkle with Spiced Pumpkin Seeds. Next, depending on how virtuous you feel, top with grated Jack cheese. Cover with 5 more tortillas. Distribute the rest of the veggies over the tortillas. Top with the remaining 5 tortillas. Cover the pies with foil and bake for 20 minutes. Remove from the oven and garnish as desired with sour cream, Green Salsa, and the remaining Spiced Pumpkin Seeds.

Serves 5 people

BLACK BEAN QUESADILLAS

These are easy to prepare and a popular lunch item at the Biscuit. We serve them topped with Chipotle Aïoli and a dollop of sour cream on the side.

1 ½ tablespoons olive oil
½ small yellow onion, minced
¾ teaspoon ground cumin
½ teaspoon dried oregano
Pinch of crushed red pepper (optional)
½ teaspoon kosher salt
2 (15 ounce) cans black beans, rinsed and drained
1 tablespoon plus 1 teaspoon masa de harina
12 eight-inch flour tortillas
2 cups grated Jack cheese

GARNISHES
Chipotle Aïoli (recipe on page 102)
Sour cream

1. Place olive oil in a large nonstick sauté pan over medium-high heat. Sauté onion, cumin, oregano, red pepper, and salt in olive oil until onions are translucent.
2. Place drained black beans in a mixing bowl. Add cooked onions and smash together with a potato masher until mixture resembles refried beans. Sprinkle masa de harina over the top of beans and stir in to incorporate.
3. Spread beans over 6 of the tortillas. Sprinkle grated Jack cheese over the beans and top each one with a second tortilla.
4. Place a griddle or sauté pan over medium-high heat. Cook the quesadillas until cheese is melted and tortillas are lightly browned on each side.
5. Serve hot, drizzled with Chipotle Aïoli. Serve sour cream on the side.

Serves 6 people as an entree, or 12 as an appetizer

EGGPLANT CHICKPEA BURGERS

These are good vegetarian burgers.

2 small eggplants
2 teaspoons salt
2 tablespoons olive oil
½ small yellow onion, minced
2 garlic cloves, minced
2 teaspoons ground cumin
1 teaspoon dried oregano
1 (15 ounce) can chickpeas, rinsed and drained
¼ cup sun-dried tomatoes in olive oil (do not drain)
½ cup grated Parmesan cheese
1 ¼ cups bread crumbs
2 teaspoons freshly ground black pepper

ASSEMBLING
6 buns
Lettuce
Sliced tomato
Tomato Coulis (recipe on page 105)

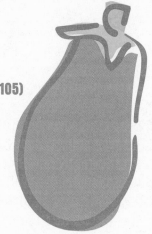

1. Peel eggplant and cut into ½-inch dice. Place in a colander and sprinkle with salt to expel excess moisture and take away bitterness. Let drain for at least 30 minutes.
2. Place a large nonstick sauté pan over medium-high heat. Add 1 tablespoon of the olive oil to the pan. Once oil is hot, add the diced eggplant, onion, garlic, cumin, and oregano. Cook until eggplant is tender and onions are translucent. Turn mixture into a large bowl and let cool slightly.
3. Place drained chickpeas in a small bowl and mash with a potato masher or the back of a fork until coarsely chopped. Add to eggplant mixture.
4. Coarsely chop sun-dried tomatoes and add to eggplant mixture. Using your hands, mix Parmesan, bread crumbs, and black pepper into the eggplant mixture. Mixture should just hold together. Form into 6 patties.
5. In large sauté pan over medium-high heat, cook the patties in the remaining tablespoon of olive oil until lightly browned on each side, about 3 to 5 minutes per side. Serve on lightly toasted buns with lettuce and tomato or Tomato Coulis.

Serves 6 people

HERBY TURKEY BURGERS

Contrary to popular belief, hamburgers are better cooked on a griddle or in a pan than grilled. If these burgers are cooked on a hot griddle that is sprinkled with salt, they will get a nice, crusty exterior and a juicy crust. Try it—you'll like it!

½ small yellow onion, minced
1 garlic clove, minced
1 tablespoon minced fresh parsley
1 tablespoon minced fresh basil
1 ½ teaspoons minced fresh rosemary
½ teaspoon kosher salt
1 teaspoon freshly ground black pepper
2 pounds lean ground turkey
2 tablespoons sour cream
1 teaspoon kosher salt for sprinkling over pan

ASSEMBLING
6 Mushy Whole-Wheat Rolls (recipe on page 69)
Lettuce
Sliced tomatoes
Roasted Red Pepper Mustard (recipe on page 103)

1. In a large mixing bowl combine onion, garlic, parsley, basil, rosemary, salt, and pepper.
2. Add ground turkey and sour cream to herb mixture. Using your hands, gently mix everything together until just incorporated. Form into 6 patties.
3. Place a griddle or heavy sauté pan over medium-high heat. Lightly sprinkle salt over the surface of the griddle. Add burgers to the griddle and cook for approximately 7 minutes on each side. (Internal temperature should reach 180°F.) Serve burgers on Mushy Whole-Wheat Rolls, with lettuce, sliced tomatoes, and Roasted Red Pepper Mustard.

Serves 6 people

RATATOUILLE, BISCUIT STYLE

We make Ratatouille at the Biscuit in 15-gallon batches. It's an enormous amount of slicing and dicing, and by the time we finish, we feel we have put everything but the kitchen sink in the pot. We serve Ratatouille as an entree—a bowl full of pasta and lots of cheese. Ratatouille tends to be even tastier the second day, so don't be afraid of having leftovers. They will be eaten.

½ cup olive oil
4 garlic cloves, minced
8 ounces button mushrooms, finely sliced
1 small yellow onion, cut into ½-inch dice
1 red bell pepper, cut into ½-inch dice
1 green bell pepper, cut into ½-inch dice
1 zucchini, cut into ½-inch dice
1 yellow squash, cut into ½-inch dice
1 small eggplant, cut into ½-inch dice
¼ cup capers
¼ cup sun-dried tomatoes, roughly chopped
¼ cup kalamata olives, pitted and roughly chopped
1½ teaspoons freshly ground black pepper
½ teaspoon crushed red pepper flakes
2 teaspoons kosher salt
2 teaspoons dried basil
1 teaspoon dried oregano
1½ teaspoons dried thyme
1 (28 ounce) can peeled Roma tomatoes with their juice
½ cup red wine
¼ cup balsamic vinegar
1 pound uncooked penne pasta
½ pound fresh buffalo mozzarella cheese, cut into ¼-inch slices

GARNISHES
Fresh basil, shredded
Freshly grated Asiago cheese

1. Place a heavy-bottomed stockpot over medium-high heat. Add olive oil. When oil is hot add garlic, mushrooms, onion, peppers, zucchini, yellow squash, and eggplant. Sauté until veggies are soft and onions are translucent. The veggies should just begin to brown.

2. Stir in the capers, sun-dried tomatoes, olives, and spices. Crush the tomatoes with a potato masher and add, juice and all, to the pot. Add red wine and balsamic vinegar, reduce heat to low, and let simmer for 1 hour to allow the flavor to develop fully.

3. Cook penne in boiling water until al dente. Drain pasta and mix with Ratatouille and buffalo mozzarella cheese. Serve topped with fresh basil and grated Asiago cheese.

Serves 6 to 8 people

LINGUINE WITH ROASTED RED PEPPER CREAM SAUCE

At the Biscuit this pasta is served topped with grilled shrimp, crumbled blue cheese, and crisp turkey bacon.

3 red bell peppers
2 cups heavy cream
Dash of Tabasco
¼ teaspoon kosher salt
¼ teaspoon white pepper
⅛ teaspoon cayenne pepper
1 pound uncooked linguine
¼ cup grated Parmesan cheese

GARNISHES
Grilled shrimp
Crumbled blue cheese
Crisp, crumbled turkey bacon

1. Place peppers under broiler or on hot grill and cook, turning frequently, until skins are blistered and peppers are charred evenly on all sides. Place peppers in a paper bag. Close the bag until peppers are cool enough to handle.
2. Gently scrape the charred skins off the outside of the peppers with the back edge of a paring knife. Remove the stems and seeds. Puree the peppers in a food processor or blender until smooth.
3. Add the cream, Tabasco, salt, white pepper, and cayenne and process.
4. Cook linguine in boiling water until al dente. Drain and set aside.
5. In a large sauté pan bring red pepper cream sauce to a simmer. Add Parmesan and toss in cooked linguine. Continue to cook until sauce is bubbly and pasta is hot. Divide pasta among individual serving dishes. Top with preferred garnishes or serve au natural.

Serves 6 people

SOUTHERN SUMMER PRIMAVERA

This pasta utilizes all the good vegetables grown in the South during the summer. It is light in calories and hearty in flavor.

1 pound uncooked fettucine
2 garlic cloves, minced
½ teaspoon crushed red pepper flakes
¼ cup olive oil
1 Vidalia onion, finely sliced
3 cups cleaned and roughly chopped mustard greens
2 cups fresh white corn kernels,
  preferably Silver Queen
2 tomatoes, peeled, seeded, and coarsely chopped
1 ½ cups black-eyed peas, cooked in simmering
  water until tender and drained
½ teaspoon kosher salt
3 tablespoons balsamic vinegar

GARNISHES
Goat cheese, preferably Georgia chèvre
Toasted Spiced Pecans

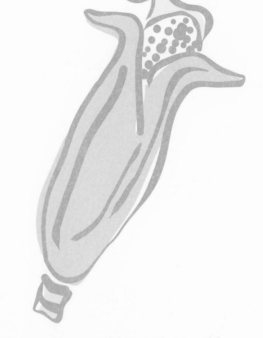

1. In a large pot of boiling water cook pasta until al dente. Drain, rinse, and set aside.
2. In a large sauté pan over medium-high heat, sauté garlic and crushed red pepper flakes in olive oil. Once the garlic reaches a golden color, add the onion, mustard greens, and corn and cook until greens begin to wilt.
3. Add the tomatoes, black-eyed peas, salt, and balsamic vinegar to the other vegetables in the sauté pan. When vegetables just begin to simmer, toss in cooked fettucine and continue to cook until all the ingredients are thoroughly heated.
4. Divide the pasta into servings and garnish each portion with a crumble of chèvre and Toasted Spiced Pecans.

TOASTED SPICED PECANS

½ cup pecan halves
1 tablespoon honey
¼ teaspoon cayenne pepper
1 teaspoon canola oil
¼ teaspoon kosher salt

Preheat oven to 350°F. Place pecans in a pie pan. Add honey, cayenne, oil, and salt to the pecans. Mix together, coating the pecans well with the spices. Bake for 7 to 10 minutes. Remove from oven and cool.

Serves 6 to 8 people

MAC AND CHEESE

Macaroni and cheese is a personal favorite. Every birthday dinner, my request was macaroni and cheese. This is a semi-spiffed-up version, but strip it down and it is the same old good eats.

8 ounces uncooked penne pasta
1 ½ cups broccoli florets or other vegetable in season,
   such as spring asparagus or summer tomatoes
4 tablespoons unsalted butter
¼ cup all-purpose flour
2 cups milk
¼ teaspoon cayenne pepper
½ teaspoon kosher salt
Dash of Tabasco
1 ½ teaspoons Worcestershire sauce
8 ounces sharp cheddar cheese, grated
¼ cup grated Parmesan cheese
4 ounces goat cheese

TOPPING
½ cup bread crumbs
2 tablespoons unsalted butter, melted and cooled
¼ cup grated Asiago cheese

1. Cook the penne pasta in boiling water until al dente. Drain and rinse with cold water. Set aside.
2. Cook the broccoli florets in boiling water until al dente. Drain, cool, and set aside.
3. Make a roux: Melt 4 tablespoons butter in a saucepan over medium heat. Whisk the flour into the butter and cook for 2 to 3 minutes, until roux is smooth and blonde in color.
4. Slowly whisk the milk into the roux and continue to cook, stirring constantly, until sauce is thick and just beginning to simmer. Remove from heat and stir in cayenne, salt, Tabasco, and Worcestershire sauce. Add sharp cheddar cheese and Parmesan and mix until well combined.
5. Preheat oven to 350°F. Combine penne, broccoli, and cheese sauce in a 2-quart baking dish. Crumble goat cheese over the top.
6. In a small bowl combine topping ingredients. Sprinkle over the top of the macaroni and cheese. Bake for 30 to 40 minutes. Cool briefly before eating. (Hot cheese is dangerous.)

Serves 6 to 8 people

ROASTED POBLANO PESTO PASTA

This pesto makes a spicy pasta sauce. If you want, you can add grilled chicken or shrimp to this dish.

3 poblano peppers
1 cup Spiced Pumpkin Seeds (recipe on page 23)
3 cups fresh cilantro leaves
2 garlic cloves, minced
½ cup crumbled feta cheese
1 cup plus 1 tablespoon olive oil
1 pound uncooked linguine
1 cup diced fresh tomatoes
1 cup fresh white corn kernels, preferably Silver Queen
¼ cup white wine

GARNISHES
¼ cup Spiced Pumpkin Seeds
  (recipe on page 23)
¼ cup crumbled feta cheese

1. Place poblano peppers over an open flame of a grill or in the broiler and cook on all sides until the skins of the peppers are blistered and charred. Place the peppers in a paper sack and allow to cool. Once cool enough to handle, scrape off the charred skin and remove the seeds and stems.
2. Place the peppers in a blender or food processor and add 1 cup of Spiced Pumpkin Seeds, cilantro, garlic, and feta cheese. Pulse, gradually adding 1 cup of olive oil. Puree until mixture resembles a coarse paste. This is the pesto.
3. Cook linguine in boiling water until al dente. Drain and rinse.
4. Place a large sauté pan over medium-high heat. Add the remaining 1 tablespoon olive oil to the pan. Once oil is hot, add tomatoes and corn. Sauté until tomatoes just begin to break down. Add pesto and white wine. Toss in pasta. (This is also the point at which you would add grilled shrimp or chicken if desired.) Cook until everything is bubbling hot. Place in serving bowls. Serve and garnish with Spiced Pumpkin Seeds and crumbled feta cheese.

Serves 4 people

CARAMELIZED ONION RASPBERRY BARBECUED CHICKEN

As strange as this recipe may sound, do not be afraid to try it. This sauce is great for grilled duck or chicken. Use a little to baste the meat, then serve the rest on the side at meal time. It is finger-licking good.

1 tablespoon canola oil
4 sweet yellow onions, cut into ¼-inch slices
¼ cup sugar
½ teaspoon chili powder
2 cups Razzberry Sauce (recipe on page 112)
½ cup raspberry vinegar
4 boneless, skinless chicken breasts
2 tablespoons canola oil for grilling

1. Place a large pan over medium-high heat and add 1 tablespoon canola oil. Once oil is bubbling hot, add onions. Cook until onions just begin to turn brown on the edges. Add sugar to the onions and continue cooking, stirring frequently to prevent burning, until onions are golden brown.

2. Add chili powder, Razzberry Sauce, and raspberry vinegar to the onions and reduce the heat so that the sauce is barely simmering. Let cook for 30 minutes to allow the flavors to develop.

3. Preheat grill until coals are white-hot. Once coals have cooled enough so that you can comfortably hold your hand 6 inches above the flame, baste the chicken with 2 tablespoons of canola oil and place on grill. Cook slowly, turning frequently. The chicken will cook fairly quickly, about 5 minutes on each side. When chicken is almost cooked, baste with barbeque sauce. Watch carefully, because the basted chicken may begin to burn if the heat is too high. Once cooked, remove from the grill and serve with additional barbeque sauce on the side for dipping.

Serves 4 people

CRAB CAKES

The fewer ingredients in a recipe, the more important it is that each ingredient be in tip-top condition. That is especially true of any seafood recipe. Give your seafood a sniff before you purchase it. Your nose is the best indicator of quality. Seafood should smell like the ocean. Anything less is unacceptable. Patience is a virtue when cleaning crabmeat. Pick through the meat very carefully to remove bits of shell. Making a good crab cake calls for a great deal of patience sometimes, but the results are well worth the effort.

1 pound lump crabmeat
1 cup bread crumbs
1 small red bell pepper
½ cup fresh white corn kernels
  (preferably Silver Queen)
⅓ cup mayonnaise
½ teaspoon kosher salt
¼ teaspoon white pepper
1 tablespoon chopped fresh parsley
1 tablespoon melted unsalted butter

GARNISH
Chipotle Beurre Blanc
  (recipe on page 106)

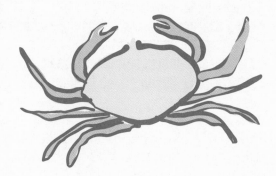

1. Pick through the crabmeat to remove any small bits of shell. Place meat in a large bowl. Add bread crumbs.
2. Cut the red pepper in half and remove the stem, seeds, and ribs. Dice pepper into ¼-inch cubes and add to the crab. With your hands, gently mix corn kernels, mayonnaise, salt, pepper, and parsley into crab.
3. Divide the crab mixture into 12 balls and lightly flatten them into cakes. Place a large sauté pan or griddle over medium heat and brush with melted butter. Add the cakes to the pan in batches and cook until golden brown, about 3 minutes per side. Serve hot, drizzled with Chipotle Beurre Blanc.

Serves 6 people

CHICKEN WITH HERB DUMPLINGS

A very satisfying dish to warm you up on a cold day.

A 3- to 4-pound fryer chicken, split
1 small onion, coarsely chopped
1 cup coarsely chopped celery
3 large carrots, coarsely chopped
5 black peppercorns
½ teaspoon kosher salt
2 teaspoons dried thyme
½ pound baby carrots, peeled
3 stalks celery, cut into ½-inch dice
1 small onion, peeled and cut into ½-inch dice
3 cups milk
1 cup heavy cream

DUMPLINGS
5 cups all-purpose flour
1 teaspoon kosher salt
1 teaspoon freshly ground black pepper
2 teaspoons finely minced fresh thyme
1 teaspoon finely minced fresh sage
½ cup vegetable shortening
1 ½ cups cold water

1. Place split chicken, coarsely chopped onion, celery, and carrots in a large stockpot, along with the peppercorns, salt, and dried thyme. Add enough water to the pot to cover the chicken and bring to a boil over high heat. Reduce the heat and cook at a simmer until the chicken is tender, about 1 hour. The meat of the chicken should fall off the bones effortlessly. Remove from heat and strain. Reserve stock and chicken and discard vegetables. Pull the meat from the bones and set aside.

2. Combine stock, chicken, baby carrots, diced celery and onions, milk, and cream in a large pot and bring to a simmer. Meanwhile, make the dumplings.

3. Combine flour, salt, pepper, and minced thyme and sage in a large bowl. Cut shortening into the flour mixture with a pastry cutter or your fingertips until mixture resembles coarse meal. Make a well in the center of the flour and add water. Gently mix with your hands until dough just pulls together into a ball. (More water may be necessary in dry weather.) On a lightly floured surface, roll dough out until it is $1/4$-inch thick. Cut dough into strips measuring 2 inches wide and 3 inches long.

4. Drop dumplings into simmering stock and cook, stirring frequently, until mixture thickens, about 35 to 45 minutes. Serve hot, with a salad and biscuit, and be fulfilled as well as full.

Serves 8 to 10 people

Savory Sides

What is served to accompany a main dish is very important. The right side dishes will complement the color, texture, and flavor of whatever they are placed with. I believe that sides are just as important as main entrees in creating a harmonious menu. Three or four deliciously prepared side dishes can stand alone and create a meal all by themselves. Fresh, seasonal, and regional vegetables are special touches to any meal. To create more of a regional southern flavor, I will sometimes cook a vegetable beyond the al dente stage. That does not mean that it is unpalatable—just a little more southern.

ROSEMARY ROASTED POTATOES

These potatoes are served with every egg dish we make at the Biscuit, and for a Saturday or Sunday brunch we roast 300 pounds of them. They go just as well with grilled fish or baked chicken and are very quick and easy to make. The seasoning, Moon Dust, is an all-purpose blend of herbs and spices that complements an array of vegetables.

3 pounds baking potatoes　　　　　**1 tablespoon chopped fresh rosemary**
4 tablespoons unsalted butter　　　**1 tablespoon Moon Dust**

1. Preheat oven to 375°F. Slice potatoes into ¼-inch-thick rounds and place in a mixing bowl.
2. Melt butter and rosemary together in a small saucepan over low heat. Allow to simmer briefly so that the rosemary can impart its flavor to the butter.
3. Toss the potatoes with the rosemary butter and Moon Dust until they are well coated.
Turn potatoes onto a baking sheet or jelly roll pan and bake for 35 to 45 minutes. Potatoes will be golden brown and crisp on the outside and tender and moist on the inside when they are ready. Serve hot out of the oven—cold roasted potatoes are just not as tasty.

Serves 6 people

MOON DUST
⅓ cup kosher salt　　　　　　　　　**¾ teaspoon dried oregano**
1 ½ teaspoons lemon pepper　　　　**¾ teaspoon dried basil**
2 ¼ teaspoons dried thyme　　　　**2 tablespoons dried rosemary**
2 ¼ teaspoons onion powder　　　**¾ teaspoon curry powder**
¾ teaspoon chili powder　　　　　**1 tablespoon Cajun spice mix**
½ teaspoon cayenne pepper　　　　**　(such as Prudhomme's Cajun Magic)**

Place all ingredients in a food processor or blender and puree to combine and grind spices. Store at room temperature for several months.

Makes ¾ cup

SAGEY APPLE TURKEY SAUSAGE

The sausage for the restaurant is made in 250-pound batches by our friend Biff Pocoroba at Sausage World. (Baseball fans may remember Biff from his days with the Atlanta Braves.) I created this recipe for at-home consumption. The fresh rosemary and sage give the sausage a wonderful aroma when it's cooking. The apples and onions help keep the sausage moist.

1 pound lean ground turkey
1 tablespoon unsalted butter
1 tablespoon minced fresh sage
1 ½ teaspoons minced fresh rosemary
1 Granny Smith apple, peeled and diced
¼ cup minced yellow onion
¼ teaspoon white pepper
¼ teaspoon cayenne pepper
½ teaspoon kosher salt
Dash of freshly grated nutmeg

1. Place ground turkey in large mixing bowl.
2. Melt butter in a medium sauté pan over medium heat. Add sage, rosemary, diced apple, and onion and cook until onions are soft and translucent. Cool mixture completely and add to turkey.
3. Season turkey with white pepper, cayenne pepper, salt, and nutmeg. Mix all ingredients by hand until just combined. Form into eight 2½-inch patties.
4. Heat a large nonstick sauté pan over medium-high heat. Cook sausage patties until lightly browned, about 3 to 5 minutes per side.

Makes 8 patties, serving 4 people

CREAMY DREAMY POLENTA

Polenta is a staple at the Biscuit. It is easy to make, and added cheeses and herbs can be altered to suit any dish. Leftovers are great too. Simply spread extra polenta into the bottom of a lightly oiled pie tin and chill. Once the polenta is cold, cut into wedges and grill or sauté. The outside will brown up nicely, and the inside will be moist and creamy. Serve this instead of grits at breakfast or as a side with dinner.

1 ½ cups water
1 ½ cups Chicken Stock (recipe on page 95)
  or Veggie Stock (recipe on page 93)
1 garlic clove, minced
½ of a small onion, minced
6 tablespoons unsalted butter
2 teaspoons kosher salt
1 serrano pepper, seeded and minced
1 teaspoon freshly ground black pepper
2 tablespoons chopped fresh rosemary
1 cup stone-ground yellow cornmeal
½ cup grated Parmesan cheese
½ cup grated mozzarella cheese
⅔ cup sour cream

1. Place water, stock, garlic, onion, butter, salt, serrano pepper, black pepper, and rosemary in a heavy-bottomed saucepan and bring ingredients to a simmer over medium heat.
2. Remove from heat and slowly whisk in cornmeal. Return to stove and cook over low heat, stirring constantly, until very thick and creamy, about 15 minutes.
3. Remove from heat and stir in Parmesan cheese, mozzarella, and sour cream. Serve hot.

Serves 6 people

PUDGE

Potatoes have always been a favorite in my family. Whether they are baked, fried, boiled, or roasted, we love them. Pudge is very simple and very satisfying. It contains no cream or butter, just a little bit of olive oil, so it is pretty good for you as well as being tasty.

3 pounds red-skinned potatoes, thinly sliced (do not peel)
1 ½ cups Chicken Stock (recipe on page 95) or Veggie Stock (recipe on page 93)
1 ½ teaspoons freshly ground black pepper
2 garlic cloves, minced
¼ cup sun-dried tomatoes in olive oil
3 tablespoons olive oil
⅔ cup grated Parmesan cheese
5 large basil leaves, finely chopped

1. Place potatoes, stock, pepper, garlic, sun-dried tomatoes, and olive oil in a large Dutch oven. Bring to a boil, reduce heat until mixture is barely simmering, cover, and cook until potatoes are very tender, about 20 minutes.
2. Remove from heat and sprinkle Parmesan cheese over potatoes. Mash with a potato masher. Stir in chopped basil and serve at once. If prepared in advance, reheat in a 350°F oven.

Serves 6 people

MAPLE-SCENTED SWEET POTATOES

Sweet potatoes are so southern and so good for you. These are sweetened with maple syrup, and the vanilla extract makes them exceptionally aromatic.

3 pounds sweet potatoes
4 tablespoons unsalted butter, at room temperature
¼ cup heavy cream
¼ cup maple syrup
1 tablespoon light brown sugar
½ teaspoon vanilla extract
½ teaspoon kosher salt
¼ teaspoon white pepper

1. Preheat the oven to 350°F. Place potatoes in a stockpot, cover with water, and boil over high heat until tender. Drain.
2. When potatoes are cool enough to handle, slip off the skins and discard. Place the meat in a large mixing bowl.
3. Add butter, cream, maple syrup, light brown sugar, vanilla, salt, and white pepper to the potatoes and whip with an electric mixer until light and fluffy. Place potatoes in an ovenproof dish and reheat for 20 minutes.

Serves 6 to 8 people

SPICY ORANGE-SCENTED COLLARD GREENS

Unlike conventional southern collard greens, these are cooked without fatback, but they are not lacking in flavor. Loaded with garlic, ginger, and orange, their fragrant aroma will entice a traditionalist to try them.

3 bunches collard greens, triple washed and stemmed
2 garlic cloves, minced
1-inch knob of fresh ginger, peeled and minced
Zest from 1 orange
Juice from 1 orange
1 small onion, thinly sliced
¼ cup soy sauce
½ teaspoon crushed red pepper flakes
1 ½ cups Chicken Stock (recipe on page 95) or Veggie Stock (recipe on page 93)

Place all ingredients in a large pot, cover, and cook over medium heat until greens are tender and wilted, about 20 minutes.

Serves 6 to 8 people

EGGPLANT PANCAKES

This is a great side dish topped with Tomato Coulis and crumbled feta cheese, or cook these up for brunch and serve them with over-easy eggs and Italian sausage. It is important to salt and drain the eggplant; otherwise the batter will not bind together well enough to cook.

2 medium-sized eggplants, peeled and cut into ¼-inch dice
1 ½ teaspoons kosher salt
1 tablespoon olive oil
½ yellow onion, cut into ¼-inch dice
2 teaspoons minced fresh oregano
¾ cup all-purpose flour
½ cup heavy cream
2 large eggs
1 tablespoon olive oil for griddle

GARNISHES
¼ cup crumbled feta cheese
¾ cup Tomato Coulis (recipe on page 105)

1. Place diced eggplant in a colander and sprinkle with kosher salt. Let drain for 20 minutes.
2. Add olive oil to a large nonstick sauté pan and place over medium-high heat. Once oil is hot, sauté eggplant, onion, and oregano until onions are translucent and eggplant is tender. Turn into a colander, drain, and cool. Once cool, place in a large mixing bowl.
3. Add flour, cream, and eggs to the cooled eggplant. Mix until well combined.
4. Place a griddle or large sauté pan over medium-high heat. Brush lightly with olive oil. Ladle pancake batter onto the griddle in ¼-cup amounts. When bubbles appear on the surface of the cakes, flip and cook until golden brown.

Makes about 20 small cakes, serving 5 to 6 people

SOUTHERN-STYLE GREEN BEANS

Because we do not cook with any pork or beef at the restaurant, it is hard to get that true southern flavor with many of our dishes. I have found that by using a few different peppers and a touch of balsamic vinegar, I can obtain a similar flavor. Do not be afraid of overcooking these beans. The longer they cook, the better they seem to taste. A little butter added at the end is the perfect finishing touch.

4 pounds snap green beans, tipped and tailed
1 small onion, finely sliced
2 garlic cloves, minced
2 teaspoons kosher salt
2 teaspoons freshly ground black pepper
1 teaspoon crushed red pepper flakes
½ teaspoon Tabasco
2 teaspoons Worcestershire sauce
2 teaspoons dried thyme
1 tablespoon balsamic vinegar
1 cup water
2 tablespoons unsalted butter

1. Place all ingredients except butter in a Dutch oven. Cook over medium heat until mixture is simmering. Reduce the heat to low and cover. Continue to cook for at least 20 minutes.
2. Remove the lid and check the beans to make sure they are tender. When they have reached the desired consistency (almost falling apart), remove from heat and add butter. Give the beans a final stir before serving to make sure all the seasonings are evenly distributed.

Serves 6 to 8 people

COCONUT CURRY RICE

Use jasmine rice for this recipe to produce a nice, sticky consistency.

4 tablespoons unsalted butter
1 small onion, minced
1 ¼ teaspoons curry powder
2 ½ cups uncooked jasmine rice
1 cinnamon stick
2 teaspoons kosher salt
2 teaspoons sugar
3 ½ cups water
1 (14 ounce) can unsweetened coconut milk

1. Place butter in a heavy-bottomed medium saucepot and melt over medium heat. Add onion and curry and cook until onion is translucent.
2. Add rice and stir to coat all the grains with butter and curry. Add the cinnamon stick, salt, sugar, water, and coconut milk to the rice. Bring to a boil, then reduce heat to a simmer. Cover and cook for 25 minutes. Rice grains will be tender, plumped, and sticky when done. Remove from heat and serve.

Serves 6 to 8 people

SAVORY CORNBREAD PUDDING

This is an excellent alternative to traditional Thanksgiving dressing. But do not save this recipe just for the holidays. It makes a great side for any roasted meat.

CORNBREAD
1 cup all-purpose flour
½ teaspoon baking soda
1 ½ teaspoons baking powder
1 tablespoon sugar
¾ teaspoon kosher salt
¾ cup yellow cornmeal
2 large eggs
1 ½ cups nonfat buttermilk
4 tablespoons unsalted butter, melted and cooled

SAVORY PUDDING
4 cups cornbread, broken into 1-inch pieces
6 tablespoons unsalted butter
2 stalks celery, minced
1 small onion, minced
1 tablespoon chopped fresh sage
2 teaspoons chopped fresh thyme
3 cups half and half
2 teaspoons kosher salt
1 teaspoons white pepper
6 large egg yolks

1. Make the cornbread. Preheat the oven to 375°F. Grease a 9 x 13-inch baking dish. Combine all the dry ingredients for the cornbread in a large bowl and make a well in the center. In a separate bowl whisk together the eggs, buttermilk, and melted butter. Pour liquid ingredients into the well and mix together until just combined. Turn batter into prepared pan and bake for 20 minutes. Remove from oven and cool. Reduce oven temperature to 350°F.
2. Crumble cornbread into a 9 x 13-inch baking dish. In a large sauté pan over medium heat, melt butter, add celery and onions to the pan, and cook until onions are translucent. Sprinkle in sage and thyme, remove from heat, and set aside to cool.
3. Whisk together half-and-half, salt, pepper, and egg yolks. Pour cooked vegetables over cornbread and add half-and-half mixture to the pan, stirring gently to combine. Cover dish with foil and bake for 30 to 40 minutes. A knife inserted in the center of the pudding will come out clean when the pudding is cooked.

Serves 8 to 10 people

WHITE BEAN CASSOULET

Ultra-rich, these beans make a decadent side dish that is slightly tangy and very fragrant. You can serve White Bean Cassoulet as a side dish or top it with grilled chicken sausage and serve it as a main dish. In a pinch, you can use three 14-ounce cans of white beans, but cooking the beans from scratch in fresh stock makes them extra tasty.

½ pound dried small white navy beans
3 cups Chicken Stock (recipe on page 95) or Veggie Stock (recipe on page 93)
2 garlic cloves, minced
2 shallots, minced
2 carrots, peeled and cut into ½-inch dice
2 tablespoons chopped fresh parsley
1 tablespoon chopped fresh rosemary
2 teaspoons kosher salt
½ teaspoon white pepper
2 tablespoons extra-virgin olive oil
1 cup Crème Fraîche (recipe on page 104)

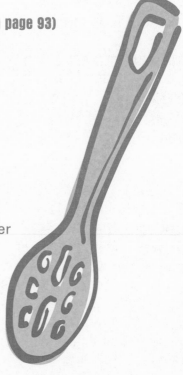

1. Place beans in a Dutch oven and add enough water to cover by 1 inch. Place over high heat and bring to a boil. Remove from heat and cover. Let sit for 1 hour.
2. Place beans in their liquid back on stove and add stock, garlic, shallots, and carrots. Bring to a low simmer and cook for 45 minutes to an hour. Beans will be tender and just starting to fall apart. Remove from heat and stir in parsley, rosemary, salt, pepper, olive oil, and Crème Fraîche. Taste for seasonings and serve.

Serves 4 people as a main course or 6 to 8 as a side dish

ARTICHOKE RISOTTO

The Italian short-grain rice called Arborio cooks up to a creamy consistency. Risotto can be flavored to complement just about any dish. Often we flavor ours with oven-roasted tomatoes or artichokes and freshly grated Asiago cheese and serve it with grilled chicken. For a more delicate flavor that goes well with seafood, replace the artichokes and cheese with a few herbs and a touch of citrus zest.

4 tablespoons unsalted butter
1 teaspoon minced fresh thyme
½ small onion, minced
½ teaspoon kosher salt
½ teaspoon white pepper
1 ½ cups Arborio rice
3 cups Chicken Stock (recipe on page 95) or Veggie Stock
  (recipe on page 93)
1 (14 ounce) can quartered artichoke hearts, drained
¼ cup freshly grated Asiago cheese
¼ cup freshly grated Parmigiano-Reggiano cheese

1. In a heavy-bottomed saucepan melt butter over medium heat. Add thyme, onion, salt, and white pepper to the butter. Cook until onions are translucent. Stir in Arborio rice, stirring to coat all the grains with the butter.
2. Add 2 cups of stock to the rice and continue to cook over medium heat, uncovered, until almost all the stock is absorbed. Add the remaining stock and cook, stirring frequently, until risotto reaches a creamy consistency and the rice is cooked through. Remove from heat.
3. Gently stir artichoke hearts and grated cheeses into the risotto and taste for seasonings. Serve hot off the stove, with extra cheese on the side if desired.

Serves 6 people

Out of the Stockpot

Soups have to be what I enjoy cooking most. Your creative instinct can take over when you make soup. A good bowl of soup can begin a fancy dinner or be a meal by itself. The base to a great soup is the stock, and the way to obtain the best flavor is to make the stock from scratch. It is not difficult and well worth the effort. An additional benefit to making your own stock is that the smell of a fresh stock simmering is a good way to get those creative juices flowing. Soups tend to taste better the second day, so don't be afraid of leftovers. They will only get better. The soups we make at the Biscuit are almost always made with vegetable stock, but if you desire a richer, heartier soup, use a chicken stock. Cook up a pot of soup and enjoy, because good soup really is good food.

SPICY BLACK BEAN SOUP

Black bean soup topped with Chipotle Aïoli and a dollop of sour cream is a one-dish meal.

1 pound dried black beans
2 tablespoons olive oil
3 garlic cloves, minced
1 small carrot, peeled and cut into ¼-inch dice
2 small onions, minced
1 stalk of celery, minced
1 teaspoon dried thyme
2 teaspoons dried oregano
2 tablespoons cumin powder
1 tablespoon chili powder
Pinch of crushed red pepper flakes
2 teaspoons kosher salt
1 (28 ounce) can of crushed tomatoes
6 cups Veggie Stock (recipe on page 93)

GARNISHES
Chipotle Aïoli (recipe on page 102)
Sour cream

1. Remove any debris or pebbles from black beans. Rinse, drain, and set aside.
2. Place olive oil in a stockpot and heat over medium-high heat. Add garlic, carrot, onions, and celery to the pot and simmer until onions start to become translucent and carrots tender. Add the thyme, oregano, cumin, chili powder, red pepper flakes, and salt and cook for another minute.
3. Place rinsed beans in the pot. Add the tomatoes and Veggie Stock and bring to a boil. Reduce the heat so that mixture is barely simmering and cover. Simmer slowly over low heat for 1 hour. Stir and add water if beans look dry. The beans should be covered with liquid and falling apart when the soup is finished. Continue to cook until beans are tender, stirring often to prevent scorching on the bottom of the pot.

4. When the beans are done, turn off the heat and cool briefly. If you want a smoother consistency, puree the soup at this point. Place in individual bowls and serve topped with Chipotle Aïoli and a dollop of sour cream.

Makes 2 ½ to 3 quarts, serving 6 to 8 people

MUSHROOM, BARLEY, AND MISO SOUP

Miso is a fermented bean paste used in Japanese cooking. The flavor is similar to a rich, concentrated soy sauce. It is also sold as red miso, which has a slightly more delicate flavor. This savory substance provides protein, aroma, and depth. Adding miso to this soup gives a rich flavor, almost as if you had used beef stock.

2 tablespoons olive oil
8 ounces button mushrooms, finely sliced
8 ounces shiitake mushrooms,
  stemmed and finely sliced
8 ounces cremini mushrooms, finely sliced
4 ounces fancy mushrooms, such as chanterelles,
  oyster mushrooms, or portobellos, finely sliced
2 teaspoons dried thyme
1 teaspoon freshly ground black pepper

½ teaspoon kosher salt
2 small carrots, peeled and cut into ¼-inch dice
2 small onions, minced
6 cups Roasted Veggie Stock (recipe on page 94)
¾ cup pearl barley
2 tablespoons red miso paste
2 teaspoons Worcestershire sauce
¼ teaspoon Tabasco
2 tablespoons chopped fresh parsley

1. Place oil in a stockpot and add all the sliced mushrooms, thyme, pepper, salt, carrots, and onions. Cook over medium heat until the mushrooms are wilted and the onions turn translucent. Add the Roasted Veggie Stock and bring to a boil. Reduce the heat to a simmer. Meanwhile, prepare the barley.

2. In a small saucepan simmer the barley in 2 cups of water for 35 to 45 minutes. When the barley is tender, add it to the mushroom soup. Stir in the miso paste, Worcestershire sauce, Tabasco, and parsley. Taste and add additional salt and pepper if desired.

3. Serve steamy hot, with a loaf of bread and a bottle of wine.

Makes 2½ quarts, serving 6 to 8 people

ZUCCHINI, TOMATO, AND ORZO SOUP

Orzo is a flat, rice-shaped pasta. When you make this soup it is important to cook the orzo and then add it to the soup only just before you are ready to serve it; otherwise it will lose its al dente texture. Although this recipe calls for canned tomatoes, use garden fresh ones when they are available in the summer.

2 tablespoons olive oil
2 garlic cloves, minced
¼ cup fresh basil leaves, coarsely chopped
4 medium-sized zucchini, cut in half lengthwise and sliced into ¼-inch crescents
1 small onion, cut into ¼-inch dice
1 (28 ounce) can diced tomatoes with their juice
6 cups Veggie Stock (recipe on page 93)
½ teaspoon kosher salt
½ teaspoon freshly ground black pepper
1 tablespoon balsamic vinegar
8 ounces uncooked orzo pasta
½ cup freshly grated Asiago cheese

1. Place oil in a stockpot and put over medium-high heat. Add garlic and basil to the hot oil and cook until garlic just begins to turn golden. Add zucchini and onion and cook until onion begins to turn translucent.
2. Stir the tomatoes into the zucchini and add the Veggie Stock. Bring soup to a boil. Season with salt, pepper, and balsamic vinegar and reduce the heat to a simmer. Cook for 20 minutes.
3. While the soup is simmering, cook orzo according to package directions. Rinse and drain. When soup is finished cooking, add prepared orzo. Place in individual bowls and serve topped with freshly grated Asiago cheese.

Makes 2½ quarts, serving 6 to 8 people

CURRIED LENTIL SOUP

When you use curry it is important that you sweat the spice in hot oil to extract its full flavor. Curry is a blend of many different spices and can vary in heat, so be careful. Lentils, like any dried legume, need to be rinsed and picked through to remove any pebbles or dirt. For a heartier soup, serve topped with grilled turkey sausage, but a vegetarian version is simply garnished with chopped parsley.

2 tablespoons olive oil
1 tablespoon curry powder
2 onions, cut into ¼-inch dice
2 carrots, cut into ¼-inch dice
2 celery stalks, thinly sliced
2 teaspoons dried thyme
2 cups lentils, rinsed
4 ½ cups Veggie Stock (recipe on page 93)
½ teaspoon kosher salt
¼ teaspoon white pepper

GARNISHES
8 ounces grilled turkey sausage, sliced
¼ cup chopped fresh parsley

1. Heat olive oil in a stockpot over medium-high heat. Add curry and cook for a few moments to release the flavors in the spice. Add the onions, carrots, and celery to the pot and cook until the onions begin to become translucent.
2. Stir the thyme and lentils into the cooked veggies. Add the Veggie Stock and bring soup to a boil. Reduce the heat so that the soup is barely simmering and cook, covered, for 35 to 45 minutes, or until the lentils are soft. Season with salt and pepper and serve hot, garnished with slices of turkey sausage and chopped parsley.

Makes 1½ to 2 quarts, serving 4 to 6 people

BISCUIT GUMBO

In addition to the vegan soups we serve on the Biscuit's daily menu, we make special soups in the fall and winter that are rich in flavor and hearty enough to be meals all on their own. This is one of them. To make a great gumbo you must have time and patience. Achieving the dark roux necessary for gumbo is an art, but getting the proper color is a necessity. One final note: It is impossible to make a small pot of gumbo, but no one ever seems to mind.

A 3-pound fryer chicken
8 tablespoons (1 stick) unsalted butter
1 cup all-purpose flour
1 onion, cut into ¼-inch dice
2 stalks celery, thinly sliced
2 green bell peppers, seeded and cut into ¼-inch dice
2 red bell peppers, seeded and cut into ¼-inch dice
4 garlic cloves, minced
½ pound okra, sliced into ½-inch-thick rings
2 tablespoons Prudhomme's Cajun Magic
1 ½ teaspoons dried thyme
1 teaspoon cayenne pepper
1 teaspoon crushed red pepper flakes
½ teaspoon kosher salt
2 teaspoons Tabasco
1 recipe Brown Chicken Stock (recipe on page 96)
1 (28 ounce) can diced tomatoes with their juice
2 cups cooked turkey sausage, cut into ¼-inch circles
1 pound shrimp, peeled and deveined
2 heaping tablespoons filé powder
2 cups cooked brown rice

1. Place chicken in a large stockpot and cover with water. Bring to a boil, then reduce the heat to a simmer. Cook for 25 minutes, or until chicken is tender and meat is falling off the bones.

Cover and cool. Once the chicken has cooled, remove the meat from the bones and refrigerate until ready to use.

2. In a stockpot over medium-high heat, melt butter. When butter is melted and bubbling, whisk in flour. Cook, stirring constantly, until roux is dark maroon in color. This will take up to 25 minutes, depending on the heat of your stove. Be patient. The darker the roux becomes, the more flavor and color the gumbo will have.

3. Carefully add the onion, celery, peppers, garlic, and okra to the pot. (The roux is very hot, so the veggies may splatter if added too quickly.) Stir until veggies are coated with the roux, then add Cajun Magic, thyme, cayenne, red pepper flakes, salt, and Tabasco. Cook until onions start to turn translucent and red and green peppers are tender. Add the Brown Chicken Stock and tomatoes and bring to a boil. Reduce the heat to a simmer and cook, stirring frequently, for 2 to 4 hours. The longer it cooks, the better it tastes.

4. Just before serving, stir in sliced sausage, shrimp, and the chicken meat. Bring mixture back to a simmer and cook until shrimp are pink and chicken hot. Sprinkle filé powder over the gumbo, give it a final stir, and serve over brown rice.

Makes 1 gallon, great for large groups of people

YELLOW TOMATO GAZPACHO

This is definitely a summer soup. Make it with garden-fresh tomatoes and chill it for several hours before serving for a cool, crisp, and spicy delight.

3 yellow tomatoes, cored and diced into 1-inch pieces
1 yellow bell pepper, seeded and cut into 1-inch pieces
2 cucumbers, peeled and cut into 1-inch pieces
1 carrot, peeled and cut into 1-inch pieces
1 stalk celery, cut into 1-inch pieces
1 serrano pepper, stemmed and minced
½ of a small red onion, minced
2 tablespoons chopped fresh cilantro
1 garlic clove, minced
1 tablespoon freshly squeezed lemon juice
2 tablespoons extra-virgin olive oil
1 ½ teaspoons balsamic vinegar
½ teaspoon kosher salt
¼ teaspoon white pepper
¼ teaspoon Tabasco

GARNISHES
Cilantro Crème Fraîche (recipe on page 104)
A few sprigs of cilantro

1. Puree the tomatoes, yellow pepper, cucumber, carrot, and celery in a food processor or blender until smooth. Place the pureed vegetables in a large bowl. Add the serrano pepper and red onion to the puree.
2. Stir the remaining ingredients into the pureed vegetables and refrigerate for at least 2 hours. The heat from the serrano will disperse through the soup as it chills and the soup will become more flavorful. Taste before serving and add additional salt and pepper if desired. Garnish with dollops of Cilantro Crème Fraîche and sprigs of cilantro.

Makes 1 ½ quarts, serving 6 people

ROASTED RED PEPPER WITH TORTELLINI SOUP

This is a hearty, rustic fall soup that will stick to your ribs.

4 red bell peppers
1 garlic clove, minced
1 onion, minced
2 tablespoons olive oil
2 tablespoons all-purpose flour
3 cups Veggie Stock (recipe on page 93)
8 ounces fresh cheese tortellini
1 cup heavy cream
½ teaspoon kosher salt
¼ teaspoon white pepper
2 tablespoons Basic Basil Pesto (recipe on page 107)

GARNISHES
½ cup freshly grated Asiago cheese
Fresh basil leaves

1. Place red peppers on a grill or broiler. Cook, turning frequently, until peppers are charred on all sides. Place the peppers in a paper sack, fold the sack, and allow peppers to steam. Once the peppers have cooled, scrape off the charred outer layers, remove the seeds and core, and puree peppers in a food processor or blender.
2. Place garlic, onion, and olive oil in a large saucepan and cook over medium-high heat until onions are translucent. Whisk in flour to form a roux and reduce the heat to low. Cook, stirring constantly, for 1 minute. Stir in pureed peppers and Veggie Stock. Bring the soup to a simmer.
3. While the soup is coming to a simmer, cook the tortellini in a separate pot according to package directions. Drain, rinse, and set aside.
4. Whisk heavy cream, salt, and white pepper into soup. Bring to a simmer and stir in pesto and cooked tortellini. Return to a simmer and remove from heat. Serve topped with Asiago cheese and fresh basil leaves.

Makes 1½ to 2 quarts, serving 6 to 8 people

CREAMY BUTTERNUT SQUASH SOUP

This is a seasonal favorite.

2 medium butternut squashes
4 tablespoons unsalted butter
1 small onion, roughly chopped
½ teaspoon ground cinnamon
¼ teaspoon ground nutmeg
¼ teaspoon cayenne pepper
½ teaspoon kosher salt
2 teaspoons minced fresh thyme
2 garlic cloves, minced
4 cups Veggie Stock (recipe on page 93) or Chicken Stock (recipe on page 95)
1 cup heavy cream

GARNISH
Spiced Pumpkin Seeds (recipe on page 23)

1. Peel, halve, and seed butternut squash. Cut the squash into 2-inch cubes.
2. Melt butter over medium heat in a large saucepan, add onion, and cook until translucent. Add the squash, spices, thyme, and garlic to the onions and cover with the stock and cream. Bring to a boil, then reduce heat to a low simmer. Cover and cook until squash is falling apart.
3. Puree the soup in batches in a blender or food processor. Taste and adjust seasonings. Serve hot, garnishing individual bowls with Spiced Pumpkin Seeds.

Makes 1½ to 2 quarts, serving 6 to 8 people

Baked Delicacies

Baking has always been my first love. I have fond memories from my childhood of making lemon meringue pie with my father and watching carefully as my mother created Danish Puff. It always seemed so mysterious. How could butter, flour, and sugar become something so magnificent? The more I baked the more I learned. I learned why gluten in flour is so important. A high-gluten bread flour is invaluable when you want a chewy texture for bread, and a soft wheat flour with lower gluten will yield a tender and flaky biscuit. I learned that sugar caramelizes baked goods, which adds color, and that fats make things tender and moist. I learned what an important role temperature and humidity play in baking by observing that when I made biscuits or bread when it rained, they would hold less liquid than on a dry day. All of the above are just simple facts. There really are not any secrets to baking, just patience, proper technique, and practice. Only by getting down and dirty with flour, butter, and sugar will you ever learn how a good biscuit dough should feel.

FLYING BISCUITS

With some hesitation, I am revealing our greatest secret: the biscuit recipe. The hesitation comes from the fact that people will realize when they read this recipe that there really is no great secret—just a lot of patience and technique. We make an average of 700 of these fluffy pups on a weekday at the Biscuit and 1,200 on a weekend day. Many different people have made the biscuits since the restaurant has been open. Our biscuiteers arrive before the break of dawn to produce these tender little morsels. If by chance you happen to drive by early some morning, you may catch a glimpse of them through the window, hunched over a table, flour everywhere. If you look even closer you might see the sparkle of the biscuit cutter and a little white ball of dough flying through the air and landing on a sheet pan, ready to be baked for our loving patrons.

3 cups all-purpose flour (a soft winter wheat flour, such as White Lily, works best)
1 tablespoon plus 1 ½ teaspoons baking powder
¾ teaspoon salt
2 tablespoons plus 1 ½ teaspoons sugar
6 tablespoons unsalted butter, at room temperature (it should be the consistency of shortening)
⅔ cup heavy cream
⅔ cup half and half
2 tablespoons half and half for brushing on top of biscuits
1 tablespoon sugar for sprinkling on top of biscuits

1. Preheat oven to 375°F. Line a sheet pan with parchment paper.
2. Place flour, baking powder, salt, and sugar in a large mixing bowl. Cut butter into ½ table-spoon-sized bits and add to the flour. Using your fingertips or a pastry cutter, work the butter into the flour mixture until it resembles coarse meal.
3. Make a well in the center of the flour and pour in all the heavy cream and the half and half. Stir the dry ingredients into the cream and mix with a wooden spoon until dough just begins to come together into a ball.
4. Turn dough onto a lightly floured surface and knead 2 or 3 times to form a cohesive mass. Do not overwork the dough. Using a rolling pin, roll the dough to a 1-inch thickness. The correct

thickness is the key to obtaining a stately biscuit. Dip a 2½-inch biscuit cutter in flour, then cut the dough. Repeat until all the dough has been cut. Scraps can be gathered together and rerolled one more time. Place the biscuits on the prepared sheet pan, leaving about ¼ inch between them. Brush the tops of the biscuits with 1 tablespoon of half and half and sprinkle with 1 tablespoon of sugar. Bake for 20 minutes. Biscuits will be lightly browned on top and flaky in the center when done.

Makes 8 to 12 biscuits, depending on the size of the cutter

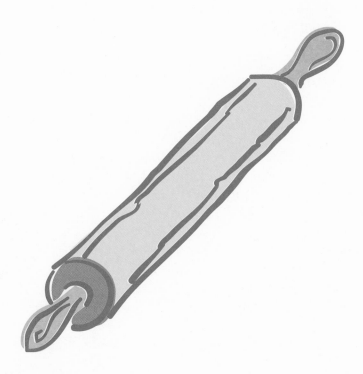

FLYING WHOLE-WHEAT BISCUITS

This is the "healthy" version of our trademark.

2 cups all-purpose flour (a soft winter wheat flour, such as White Lily, works best)
½ cup whole-wheat flour
1 ½ tablespoons baking powder
2 tablespoons sugar
1 teaspoon salt
8 tablespoons (1 stick) unsalted butter, at room temperature
  (it should be the consistency of shortening)
1 cup half and half
3 tablespoons half and half for brushing on top of biscuits
2 tablespoons sugar for sprinkling on top of biscuits

1. Preheat oven to 375°F. Line a sheet pan with parchment paper.
2. Place flour, whole-wheat flour, baking powder, sugar, and salt in a large mixing bowl. Cut in butter with your fingertips or a pastry cutter until mixture resembles coarse meal.
3. Make a well in the center of the dry ingredients. Add half and half and stir with a large spoon until mixture just begins to come together into a ball.
4. Turn dough onto a lightly floured surface and knead briefly to form a cohesive mass. Using a rolling pin, roll the dough to a 1-inch thickness and cut with a 2½-inch biscuit cutter. Dip the cutter in flour between biscuits to keep it from compressing the dough.
5. Place biscuits on prepared sheet pan so that they are almost touching. Brush tops of biscuits with 3 tablespoons of half and half and sprinkle with 2 tablespoons of sugar. Bake for 15 to 20 minutes, or until lightly browned.

Makes 10 to 12 biscuits, depending on the size of the cutter

SOUR CREAM POTATO BREAD

This soft white bread is perfect for everything from peanut butter and jelly sandwiches to stuffed French toast. Be careful. If you start eating this bread hot from the oven, before you know it, it will be gone.

1 medium baking potato, peeled and diced
1 ½ tablespoons active dry yeast
¾ cup warm water (about 98°F)
2 tablespoons sugar

1 ½ cups sour cream
¼ teaspoon baking soda
2 teaspoons salt
6 cups bread flour

1. Place diced potato in a small saucepan and cover with water. Cover and simmer until tender, about 20 minutes. Drain, mash, and cool.
2. Place yeast in the bottom of a mixing bowl to proof. Test water to make sure it is not too hot. It should feel lukewarm to the touch and measure no more than 100°F. Add the water to the yeast. Yeast should bubble to the surface and mixture should become foamy. Once this has occurred, add sugar.
3. Meanwhile combine mashed potato, sour cream, and baking soda. Add to the proofed yeast. Combine salt and bread flour in a separate bowl.
4. Place the yeast mixture in the bowl of an electric stand mixer with a dough hook. With the machine on low speed, add the flour to the yeast mixture 1 cup at a time. When dough pulls together into a ball, increase the speed to medium-low and knead the dough for 8 to 10 minutes. Turn dough into a lightly greased bowl and let rise until doubled in bulk, about 1 hour.
5. Punch dough down and divide in half. Form into 2 loaves and place in lightly greased 9 x 3-inch loaf pans. Let rise again until doubled in bulk, about 30 minutes.
6. Preheat oven to 350°F. Bake loaves for 35 to 40 minutes. When they are done, the tops of the loaves will be lightly brown, and the bottom of the loaves will have a hollow sound when thumped.

Makes 2 loaves

MUSHY WHOLE-WHEAT BREAD

This bread is made with what is called a sponge. The sponge is an initial fermentation that is made separately from the bread dough. This first fermentation gives the bread a head start. The bread will rise quickly and have a nice, yeasty flavor because of the yeast developments in the sponge. This recipe makes two loaves.

SPONGE
1 ½ tablespoons active dry yeast
2 cups warm water (about 98°F)
3 tablespoons molasses
4 cups all-purpose flour

DOUGH
3 tablespoons dark brown sugar
2 tablespoons unsalted butter, at room temperature
¾ cup milk, heated to lukewarm
1 ½ cups whole-wheat flour
2 ¼ cups bread flour
A scant 1 tablespoon salt

1. To make the sponge, place yeast in bottom of mixing bowl. Measure water and test temperature. It should be warm to the touch but not hot—98°F is good. (If your body temperature is 98.6°F, then the water should feel lukewarm to your skin.) Add the water to the yeast and stir to dissolve. Add the molasses. Let this mixture rest. The yeast will begin to bubble to the surface and the mixture will become foamy. Stir in the all-purpose flour and mix until smooth. Cover and let the sponge rise until doubled in bulk, about 30 minutes.
2. Place the sponge in the bowl of an electric stand mixer with a dough hook. With the machine on low speed, add in brown sugar and butter. Add the milk. In a separate bowl combine the whole-wheat flour, bread flour, and salt. Add to the sponge. Knead the dough on medium-low speed for 8 minutes. Turn dough into a lightly oiled bowl and let rise until doubled in bulk, about 30 minutes.

3. Preheat the oven to 350°F. Punch the dough down and divide in half. Form into 2 loaves and place in two 9 x 3-inch greased loaf pans. (You can also form the dough into rolls.) Cover loaves with a towel and let rise for the third time until doubled in bulk, about 45 minutes. Bake for 35 to 40 minutes. When they are done, loaves will be golden brown and have a nice hollow sound when you thump them.

Makes 2 loaves

MUSHY WHOLE-WHEAT ROLLS
If making rolls, form the dough into 12 balls instead of 2 loaves. Place on parchment-lined baking sheets, 3 inches apart, and let rise until doubled in bulk. Bake for 20 minutes.

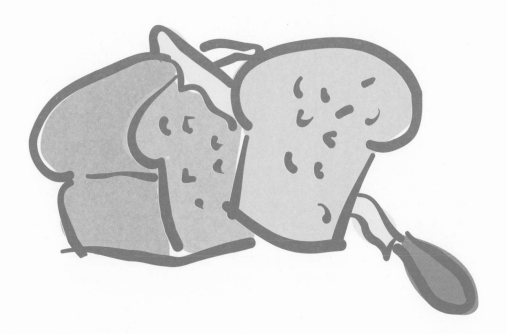

OATMEAL CRAISIN SCONES

Tender and tasty, these are a variation of the traditional scone recipe. Scones are similar to biscuits yet different in that they are sweeter and almost always contain dried fruit.

1 ½ cups all-purpose flour
½ cup organic rolled oats
1 tablespoon baking powder
1 teaspoon salt
⅓ cup (5⅓ tablespoons) unsalted butter
½ cup dried craisins
1 large egg
½ cup heavy cream
2 tablespoons unsalted butter, melted and cooled
2 tablespoons raw sugar

1. Preheat oven to 400°F. Combine flour, oats, baking powder, and salt in a large bowl. Using fingertips or a pastry cutter, cut ⅓ cup butter into the dry ingredients until mixture resembles coarse meal. Stir in craisins.
2. In a second bowl whisk together the egg and cream. Add to the scone batter and stir with a wooden spoon until just blended. Turn mixture out onto a lightly floured surface and pat with your hands into a circle approximately 9 inches in diameter. Cut into 8 pie-shaped wedges and arrange on a baking sheet so that they are spaced 1 inch apart. (Placing them close together increases the steam they release in the oven, thus helping them to rise better.)
3. Brush with melted butter and sprinkle with raw sugar. Bake 10 to 12 minutes. Scones will be lightly golden when done. These are best served hot out of the oven with Cranberry Apple Butter (page 109) or au natural.

Makes 8 scones

DANISH PUFFS

This is an old family recipe. My mother has been making Danish Puffs for special occasions ever since I can remember. This recipe can be made fairly quickly from ingredients that are probably already in your pantry. The Danish is best when eaten the day it is made.

CRUST
1 cup all-purpose flour
8 tablespoons (1 stick) unsalted butter, at room temperature
2 tablespoons water

FILLING
8 tablespoons (1 stick) unsalted butter
1 cup water
1 teaspoon almond extract
1 cup all-purpose flour
3 large eggs

GLAZE
⅓ cup confectioners' sugar
2 tablespoons heavy cream
¼ teaspoon vanilla extract
½ cup toasted sliced almonds
1 cup fresh raspberries

1. Preheat oven to 350°F. Make the crust. Place flour in a medium bowl. Using a pastry cutter or your fingertips, cut butter into the flour until mixture resembles coarse meal. Sprinkle with water and mix together with a fork. Gather mixture into a ball and divide in half. Pat each half into a 12 x 3-inch strip. Use the heel of your hand to push the dough into the right shape. (The warmth from your hands will help make the dough easier to form.) Place on a 13 x 11-inch ungreased baking sheet. Leave approximately 3 inches between the strips on the sheet pan.
2. Make the filling. Place butter and water in a heavy-bottomed saucepan and bring to a simmer. Remove from the heat and add almond extract. Whisk in flour quickly to prevent lumping. When smooth, add eggs one at a time, beating well after each egg is added. Divide the filling in half and spread over each crust, leaving ¼ inch of crust all around. Bake for 1 hour. Cool.
3. Make the glaze. Whisk together confectioners' sugar, cream, and vanilla until smooth. Drizzle over cooled Danish Puffs and sprinkle toasted almonds and raspberries over the tops.

Makes 2 Danish Puffs, serving 8 to 10 people

LOW-FAT BANANA MUFFINS

This is a low-fat version of an old favorite, but you would never know it.

1 ¼ cups mashed ripe bananas
¾ cup sugar
⅔ cup low-fat vanilla yogurt
4 ½ tablespoons unsalted butter, melted and cooled
½ teaspoon vanilla extract
2 large eggs
2 ⅔ cups all-purpose flour
¾ teaspoon baking powder
1 teaspoon baking soda
¼ teaspoon salt

1. Preheat oven to 350°F. Lightly grease a dozen muffin tins or line with paper cups. Place bananas, sugar, yogurt, melted butter, vanilla, and eggs together in a large mixing bowl and beat with a wooden spoon until smooth.
2. In a second bowl sift together flour, baking powder, baking soda, and salt. Add dry ingredients to wet and mix until just combined. Do not overmix, or the muffins will be tough.
3. Using an ice-cream scoop, fill prepared muffin pans three-quarters of the way full. Bake for 25 to 35 minutes. A toothpick inserted in the center of the muffins will come out clean when they are cooked. Remove from oven and cool slightly before eating. Hot muffins are dangerous!

Makes 1 dozen muffins

FAT-FREE GINGER CRAISIN MUFFINS

These muffins have a following at the Biscuit. They have no fat, and as a result have a chewy consistency. If you let them sit for a day they become more tender and moist. These are reminiscent of gingerbread, with a tart little punch from the craisins.

4 prunes
¼ cup water
½ cup maple syrup
½ cup molasses
6 large egg whites
½ cup nonfat buttermilk
2 ⅓ cups all-purpose flour
1 ½ teaspoons baking soda
¾ teaspoon ground ginger
¼ teaspoon ground cinnamon
¼ teaspoon ground cloves
½ cup dried craisins

1. Place prunes in a small saucepan with water and cook, covered, over low heat until prunes are plumped. Remove from heat and puree, liquid and all, in a blender or food processor.
2. Preheat oven to 350°F. Place paper muffin liners in 12 tins and lightly spray with nonstick cooking spray.
3. In a large mixing bowl whisk together prune puree, maple syrup, molasses, egg whites, and buttermilk until all ingredients are combined. In a separate bowl, sift flour, baking soda, and spices together and add to prune mixture. Stir until just combined. (Do not overmix.) Fold in craisins.
4. Using an ice-cream scoop, fill prepared cups two-thirds of the way full with batter. Bake for 25 to 35 minutes. A toothpick inserted into the center of the muffins will come out clean when they are cooked.

Makes 1 dozen muffins

OLD-FASHIONED BLUEBERRY OATMEAL MUFFINS

For professional-looking muffins, use an ice-cream scoop to fill muffin cups with batter.

½ cup organic rolled oats
1 cup nonfat buttermilk
½ cup canola oil
2 large eggs
½ cup dark brown sugar
1 ½ cups all-purpose flour
2 ½ teaspoons baking powder
¾ teaspoon ground cinnamon
¾ teaspoon baking soda
½ teaspoon salt
1 ½ cups fresh blueberries

STREUSEL TOPPING
⅔ cup all-purpose flour
⅔ cup dark brown sugar
⅓ cup organic rolled oats
6 tablespoons unsalted butter, at room temperature

1. Combine oats and buttermilk in medium bowl. Let soak for 30 minutes.
2. Preheat oven to 350°F. Lightly grease a 12-cup muffin tin.
3. Add canola oil, eggs, and brown sugar to oat mixture. Beat with a wooden spoon for 1 minute.
4. Sift together flour, baking powder, cinnamon, baking soda, and salt. Add to oat mixture and stir until just combined. Fold blueberries into batter.
5. In a separate bowl place all streusel ingredients. Use your fingertips to cut butter into the dry ingredients. Mixture will resemble coarse meal.
6. Using an ice-cream scoop, fill muffin cups three-fourths full with batter. Sprinkle streusel topping over batter. Bake 25 to 30 minutes, or until centers of muffins spring back when touched.

Makes 1 dozen muffins

BLUE CORN MUFFINS

Make these to go with soup, or serve them with jam at breakfast. They are extremely moist and will surprise everyone with their beautiful color. If blue cornmeal is unavailable, yellow will do.

2 large eggs
1 cup nonfat buttermilk
6 tablespoons unsalted butter, melted and cooled
1 ¼ cups all-purpose flour
¾ cup blue cornmeal
¼ cup sugar
⅓ cup lightly toasted pine nuts
2 teaspoons baking powder
½ teaspoon baking soda
¼ teaspoon salt

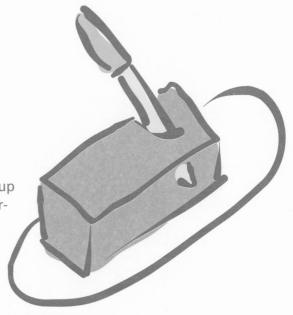

1. Preheat oven to 400°F. Lightly grease a 12-cup muffin tin. In a mixing bowl whisk eggs, buttermilk, and butter until frothy.

2. In a large mixing bowl combine flour, blue cornmeal, sugar, pine nuts, baking powder, baking soda, and salt. Make a well in the center of dry ingredients and add the buttermilk mixture. Stir until just combined.

3. Fill muffin cups level with the top of the pan. You should have enough batter to fill 8 to 10 cups. Bake for 20 minutes. Test for doneness. Muffins should spring back when lightly touched in the center. Serve hot, with Strawberry Rhubarb Jam (page 110).

Makes 8 to 10 muffins

CHOCOLATE BROWNIE PIE

This is one of the few desserts we have been making since the restaurant opened. Served warm, with a scoop of vanilla bean ice cream and a puddle of Extra-Rich Chocolate Sauce, it is the essence of comfort. Indulge and feed your soul.

PECAN CRUST
¾ cup finely ground pecans
8 tablespoons (1 stick) unsalted butter, at room temperature
¼ cup sugar
1 large egg yolk
¼ teaspoon almond extract
1 ½ cups all-purpose flour

BROWNIE FILLING
¾ cup unsweetened Dutch-process cocoa powder
2 ½ sticks (1 ¼ cups) unsalted butter, melted and cooled
4 large eggs
2 cups sugar
½ teaspoon vanilla extract
¾ cup all-purpose flour
½ cup coarsely chopped pecans

1. Preheat oven to 350°F. Make the crust. Place ground pecans, butter, and sugar in the bowl of an electric mixer and cream until light and smooth. Add the egg yolk and almond extract and pulse to combine. Pulse in flour until mixture just holds together. Press dough into the bottom and sides of a 10-inch deep-dish pie pan. Line the crust with parchment paper and weigh it down with pie weights or dry beans. Bake for 10 minutes. Remove from oven and take out pie weights and paper, return crust to oven, and bake an additional 5 minutes to crisp. Let crust cool while making the filling.
2. Whisk cocoa powder into butter until mixture is smooth. Set aside. Place eggs and sugar in the bowl of an electric mixer and beat until light and thick. Add vanilla. Add cocoa mixture

alternately with flour in 3 batches, beating briefly to combine after each addition. When just combined, fold in pecans.

3. Pour filling into prepared pie shell and bake in preheated oven for 35 to 45 minutes. Pie should just begin to crack on the top, but be soft in the center. Remove from oven and cool slightly before serving.

Makes one 10-inch pie

CREAM CHEESE COFFEE CAKE

Sweets were always a favorite at my family's gatherings. This recipe came from my Aunt Cherie, who was notorious for fattening up the family for the holidays. Although this is not a low-fat recipe, it is a family favorite, and we still make it for our loved ones to enjoy and indulge in. It has also found critical acclaim at the Biscuit. In the summer, sprinkle fresh blueberries over the cream cheese filling for an extra-special touch.

CAKE BATTER
2 sticks (1 cup) unsalted butter, at room temperature
1 cup sugar
2 large eggs
2 cups all-purpose flour
2 teaspoons baking powder
½ teaspoon salt

CAKE FILLING
2 (8 ounce) packages cream cheese, at room temperature
1 large egg yolk
½ cup sugar
1 teaspoon vanilla extract

CAKE TOPPING
¼ cup sugar
½ cup all-purpose flour
4 tablespoons unsalted butter, at room temperature

1. Preheat oven to 350°F. Lightly grease a 9 x 13-inch baking pan. Set aside.
2. Make the cake batter. In a large bowl cream butter and sugar together with an electric mixer until smooth. Add eggs one at a time, scraping the bowl well after each addition. Sift the flour, baking powder, and salt together and add to butter mixture. Beat until flour is incorporated and batter is thick, pale, and creamy. Set aside.

3. Make the cake filling. Using an electric mixer, combine all ingredients. Mix until sugar is dissolved and filling is smooth.

4. Make cake topping. Combine sugar and flour in a small bowl. Using a pastry cutter or your fingertips, cut butter into sugar and flour until mixture is crumbly. Set aside.

5. Spread two-thirds of the cake batter over the bottom of the prepared baking pan. Spread the cake filling over the cake batter. Using a large spoon, evenly distribute remaining cake batter over filling in dollops. Sprinkle entire cake surface with cake topping. Bake for 45 minutes.

Serves and satisfies the masses

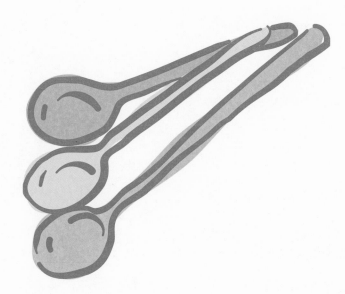

WHITE CHOCOLATE BANANA CREAM PIE

At first glance this recipe may appear too complicated. Don't be discouraged. The end results are well worth it. If you are feeling really decadent, serve each piece with an extra dollop of whipped cream on top.

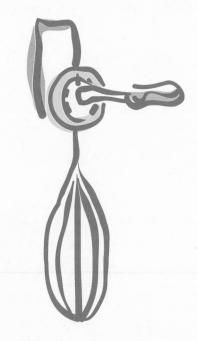

FILLING
¼ cup banana liqueur
4 tablespoons unsalted butter
2 cups half and half
½ cup sugar, divided
5 large egg yolks
½ cup cornstarch
2 ½ ounces white chocolate, finely chopped
1 teaspoon vanilla extract
1 cup heavy cream
3 ripe bananas
Additional whipped cream for topping (optional)

CRUST
1 ½ cups graham cracker crumbs
⅓ cup sugar
6 tablespoons unsalted butter, melted and cooled

1. In a medium saucepan combine banana liqueur, butter, half and half, and ¼ cup of the sugar. Place egg yolks, cornstarch, and remaining ¼ cup of sugar in mixing bowl and whisk together until smooth.

2. Bring ingredients in saucepan to a simmer over low heat. Turn off heat. Remove 1 cup of liquid from saucepan and whisk into egg yolk mixture in the bowl. (This will temper eggs and keep them from scrambling.) Add ingredients in bowl back into ingredients in saucepan. Cook over medium heat until filling is thick and bubbling, stirring constantly. Remove from heat and whisk in white chocolate and vanilla. Cover and refrigerate banana cream filling until mixture is cold to the touch.

3. Preheat oven to 350°F.

4. Make crust. Combine graham cracker crumbs, sugar, and melted butter. Press mixture into the bottom of a 10-inch deep-dish pie pan. Bake for 10 minutes, or until lightly browned. Cool completely.

5. Whip heavy cream until it forms soft peaks. Place cold banana cream filling in a large bowl and whisk until smooth and creamy. Fold in whipped cream.

6. Slice bananas and arrange over bottom of pie crust. Top with banana cream filling. Chill for at least 30 minutes before serving. Top with additional whipped cream, if desired.

Makes one 10-inch pie

KEY LIME PIE

My mother tested and retested every Key lime pie recipe available when I was a kid. This one has always been the favorite. Legend has it that Key lime pie was a dessert created in Florida during the Depression. All the ingredients were fairly easy to come by. This and our biscuit recipe are the most requested from the restaurant. They are also two of the easiest, but both rely on top-quality ingredients for excellent results. The lime juice should be freshly squeezed. If you choose to use true Key limes, whick are much more acidic than regular limes and very bitter, reduce the amount of lime juice to 1/3 cup. By the way, real Key lime pie is not green.

GRAHAM CRACKER CRUST
1 1/2 cups graham cracker crumbs
1/3 cup sugar
6 tablespoons unsalted butter, melted and cooled

FILLING
2 cups heavy cream
1 teaspoon freshly grated lime zest
1/2 cup fresh lime juice (about 4 large limes)
1 (14 ounce) can sweetened condensed milk

1. Make the crust. Preheat oven to 350°F. Combine graham cracker crumbs, sugar, and butter in a mixing bowl. Turn into a 9-inch pie pan and press ingredients firmly up the sides of the pan, covering entire surface. Bake for 7 to 10 minutes. Remove from oven and cool completely.
2. Make the filling. Whip heavy cream to soft peaks and set aside. In a large mixing bowl combine lime zest, lime juice, and condensed milk. Whisk together until mixture is slightly thickened and well combined. Add two-thirds of the whipped cream to the lime mixture and gently fold to combine. Refrigerate remaining one-third of whipped cream. Pour pie filling into prepared crust and place pie in the freezer for at least 2 hours so that it will be firm enough to cut when ready to serve. Remove from the freezer 15 to 20 minutes before serving and top with the remaining one-third of whipped cream.

Makes one 9-inch pie

FLOURLESS CHOCOLATE TORTE

Make this flourless chocolate cake with any ground nut you prefer. Top it with the Ganache Glaze given here or simply dust it with powdered sugar and serve with fresh Razzberry Sauce. Use the best quality chocolate you can find and melt it in a double boiler, well above barely simmering water. One helpful hint: Chocolate melts at 86.6°F, so it should feel cool to the touch when you heat it. Using this technique will always yield a smooth, shiny chocolate.

8 ounces bittersweet chocolate
2 sticks (1 cup) unsalted butter
¾ cup sugar

3 large eggs, separated
¾ cup finely ground almonds or other nuts
¼ cup Grand Marnier

1. Preheat oven to 350°F. Butter and lightly flour a 9-inch cake pan. Melt chocolate and butter in the top of a double boiler set over barely simmering water. Remove from heat and set aside. In a mixing bowl beat sugar and egg yolks together with a whisk until light and fluffy. Place egg whites in an impeccably clean bowl and whip to soft peaks with a clean wire whisk.
2. Using a wire whisk, fold egg yolk mixture into melted chocolate mixture. Next fold in ground nuts, then egg whites, and lastly Grand Marnier. Pour into prepared cake pan and bake for 20 minutes. Remove cake from the oven while it is still soft in the center. Place on a rack and cool completely. Turn cake onto a serving platter and ice with Ganache Glaze.

GANACHE GLAZE
¼ cup heavy cream
4 ounces bittersweet chocolate, chopped very fine

Place cream in a heavy-bottomed saucepan and bring to a simmer. Remove from heat and stir in chopped chocolate. Stir until the mixture is smooth and all the chocolate has melted. Cool slightly and pour over cooled cake.

Makes one 9-inch cake

PUMPKIN CHEESECAKE WITH PECAN CRUST

Every fall, as the holidays approach, I get requests for this cheesecake. A good cheesecake takes time to prepare, but it feeds many people because it is so rich. Instead of making the obligatory pumpkin pie for Thanksgiving, give this a try.

CRUST
1 cup all-purpose flour
2 tablespoons sugar
6 tablespoons unsalted butter
½ cup ground pecans
1 large egg yolk
2 tablespoons cold water

FILLING
5 large eggs, separated
1 cup brown sugar
1 ¼ cups sour cream
¼ teaspoon salt
1 teaspoon vanilla extract
1 teaspoon ground cinnamon
½ teaspoon ground nutmeg
3 (8 ounce) packages cream cheese, softened
1 (15 ounce) can pumpkin puree
½ cup sugar

1. Make the crust. Butter the sides and bottom of a 10-inch springform pan. In a mixing bowl combine flour and sugar. Using a pastry cutter or your fingertips, cut butter into flour until it resembles coarse meal. Stir in ground pecans. Whisk egg yolk with 2 tablespoons of water. Gently work yolk mixture into flour mixture until it just begins to bind together. Gather dough into a ball and wrap in plastic wrap. Chill for 30 minutes.
2. Preheat oven to 350°F. Press crust mixture into the bottom of prepared pan. Bake for 15 minutes.

Set aside to cool.

3. Make the filling. Whisk egg yolks, brown sugar, sour cream, salt, vanilla, cinnamon, and nutmeg together in a large mixing bowl. Set aside. Using an electric mixer, beat cream cheese until smooth. Beat in pumpkin puree. In a clean bowl, beat egg whites with sugar until soft peaks form. Fold yolk mixture into cream cheese-pumpkin mixture. When almost incorporated, gently fold in egg whites. Pour filling into pan. Wrap the entire bottom of the pan with foil and secure with a rubber band. Place springform pan in a larger pan that is at least 2 inches deep and fill larger pan with water halfway up the sides of the springform pan.

4. Place pan in preheated oven and bake for 50 minutes. Turn off the oven and leave cake in oven to cool for 1 hour. Refrigerate for several hours—overnight is best.

Makes one 10-inch cake, serving 12 to 16 people

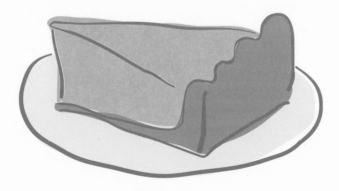

PEACH BLUEBERRY COBBLER

When the middle of the summer sets in down south, peaches and blueberries are at the height of their season. When cooked together, they create a fragrant, sweet, and bubbling stew. Serve this cobbler warm, topped with vanilla bean ice cream, and it will make the heat of summer feel like it is worthwhile.

2 cups fresh blueberries, washed and dried
1 ½ pounds fresh cling-free peaches,
  peeled and thinly sliced
¼ cup all-purpose flour
⅔ cup sugar
¼ teaspoon ground nutmeg

TOPPING
2 cups all-purpose flour
1 tablespoon plus 1 teaspoon baking powder
½ teaspoon salt
3 tablespoons sugar
4 tablespoons unsalted butter, at room temperature
1 cup heavy cream
2 tablespoons raw sugar for sprinkling over the top

1. Preheat oven to 375°F. In a large bowl mix together blueberries, peaches, flour, sugar, and nutmeg. Turn fruit into a 2-quart baking dish.
2. Make the topping. Place flour, baking powder, salt, and sugar in a mixing bowl. Cut butter into ½-tablespoon-sized pieces and work into the flour with your fingertips or a pastry cutter until mixture resembles coarse meal. With a wooden spoon, stir in cream and mix until just combined. Using a tablespoon, drop batter over the top of fruit until entire surface is covered. Sprinkle with raw sugar.
3. Bake cobbler for 40 to 50 minutes. The top will be golden and the center bubbling when done. Serve warm, with a scoop of vanilla bean ice cream.

Serves 6 to 8 people

APPLE CRISP

We make a great many cobblers and crisps at the restaurant because they are so much easier to make than pies or tarts. During apple season, this is a wonderful way to take advantage of this versatile fruit.

6 Granny Smith apples, peeled, cored, and finely sliced
½ cup sugar
1 ½ tablespoons all-purpose flour
1 teaspoon ground cinnamon
¼ teaspoon ground nutmeg
Pinch of ground cloves

CRISP TOPPING
1 cup dark brown sugar
8 tablespoons (1 stick) unsalted butter,
  at room temperature
1 cup all-purpose flour
½ cup organic rolled oats
½ cup chopped pecans
½ teaspoon ground cinnamon

1. Preheat oven to 350°F. In a large bowl combine apples, sugar, flour, cinnamon, nutmeg, and cloves. Turn apple mixture into a 9 x 13-inch baking dish.
2. Make the topping. Place brown sugar, butter, flour, oats, pecans, and cinnamon in a mixing bowl and work together with fingertips until mixture is combined into crumbly pieces (about ¼ inch in size).
3. Distribute the topping over the apples and bake for 35 to 45 minutes. Serve hot, with vanilla bean ice cream.

Serves 6 to 8 people

GINGER SNAPS

The Biscuit has made this recipe from my mother-in-law famous. At the restaurant, we make these cookies about four times their originally intended size. No one seems to mind. This recipe will yield 2 1/2 dozen regular-sized cookies. For Biscuit-sized ones, form the dough into balls with an ice-cream scoop. Be sure to refrigerate the dough for these cookies before baking them. Otherwise they will spread too much.

1 cup sugar
3/4 cup vegetable shortening
1/4 cup light molasses
1 large egg
2 cups all-purpose flour
2 teaspoons baking soda
1/4 teaspoon salt
1 teaspoon ground cinnamon
1 teaspoon ground cloves
1 teaspoon ground ginger
1/2 cup additional sugar for rolling the cookies in

1. Using an electric mixer, cream sugar and shortening until light and fluffy. Mix in molasses, then egg, scraping the bowl well between additions.
2. Sift together flour, baking soda, salt, cinnamon, cloves, and ginger. Add to the creamed mixture and mix until just combined. Chill dough for several hours.
3. Preheat oven to 375°F. Form dough into 1 1/2- to 2-inch balls. Roll the balls in sugar and place 2 inches apart on a lightly greased cookie sheet. Bake for 8 minutes. When done, the surface of the cookies will crack, and they will be crisp on the edges.

Makes 2 1/2 to 3 dozen cookies

DROP-DEAD DECADENT DOUBLE CHOCOLATE CHIP COOKIES

These cookies are every chocolate lover's dream. They remind me of chocolate truffles. Crisp on the edges yet chewy in the center, with melting bits of chocolate morsels, they are a little bite of heaven on earth.

1 ½ cups all-purpose flour
1 ½ teaspoons baking powder
¼ teaspoon salt
8 tablespoons (1 stick) unsalted butter,
  at room temperature
1 cup dark brown sugar
2 teaspoons vanilla extract
2 large eggs
16 ounces semisweet chocolate chips, divided
1 tablespoon unsalted butter
1 cup confectioners' sugar for rolling cookies in

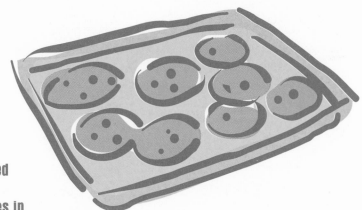

1. In a medium bowl sift together flour, baking powder, and salt.
2. With an electric mixer beat butter until smooth. Add brown sugar and vanilla and beat until light and fluffy. Add the eggs, one at a time, and mix until just combined, scraping the bowl before and after each egg is added. Add sifted flour mixture and mix on low speed until just combined.
3. In a double boiler over barely simmering water, melt 12 ounces of the chocolate chips with 1 tablespoon of butter. Cool slightly. When cool to the touch, add to the creamed mixture. Fold remaining chocolate chips into the batter and refrigerate for 1 hour.
4. Preheat oven to 350°F. Roll chilled cookie dough into 1- to 2-inch balls, then roll the balls in confectioners' sugar to lightly dust them. Place balls 2 inches apart on an ungreased cookie sheet and bake until the balls flatten slightly, about 10 to 12 minutes.

Makes 2 to 3 dozen cookies

LUSCIOUS LINZER COOKIES

These little jewels are vegan. Fill them with a good raspberry jam and you have sweet, nutty morsels.

1 cup organic rolled oats
1 cup whole unblanched almonds
1 cup all-purpose flour
½ teaspoon ground cinnamon
½ cup maple syrup
½ cup canola oil
1 teaspoon vanilla extract
1 cup raspberry jam

1. Preheat oven to 350°F. Place oats, almonds, and flour in a food processor and process until mixture resembles coarse meal. Place in a large mixing bowl and stir in cinnamon.
2. Whisk together maple syrup, canola oil, and vanilla. Make a well in the center of the dry ingredients and stir in the syrup and oil mixture with a wooden spoon until all ingredients are incorporated.
3. Form dough into 1½-inch balls. Place on a baking sheet 2 inches apart and flatten slightly. Place a thumb in the center of each cookie and push down to form an indention to hold 1 teaspoon of jam. Fill the thumb prints with jam and bake for 8 to 10 minutes.

Makes 1½ to 2 dozen cookies

OATMEAL CHOCOLATE CHIP MACADAMIA NUT COOKIES

This is our customers' favorite cookie at the Biscuit. We make these about 6 inches in diameter—quite imposing. You may wish to make them a little smaller, but if you do want gargantuan cookies, simply form the dough with an ice-cream scoop instead of a tablespoon.

2 sticks (1 cup) unsalted butter
1 cup granulated sugar
1 cup dark brown sugar
2 large eggs
½ teaspoon vanilla extract
2 ½ cups organic rolled oats
2 cups all-purpose flour
1 teaspoon baking powder
1 teaspoon baking soda
½ teaspoon salt
12 ounces semisweet chocolate chips
1 ½ cups macadamia nuts

1. Preheat oven to 350°F. In a large bowl cream butter, sugar, brown sugar, eggs, and vanilla with an electric mixer until light and fluffy.
2. Place oats in a food processor or blender and process until it resembles coarse meal. Combine ground oats, flour, baking powder, baking soda, and salt and add to the creamed butter and eggs. Gently combine with mixer on low speed, scraping the bowl frequently. Do not over-mix. Stir in chocolate chips and macadamia nuts.
3. Form dough into balls. (We make them tennis ball-sized, but you can make them golf ball-sized if you desire more and smaller cookies.) Place 3 inches apart on an ungreased cookie sheet and bake for 8 to 10 minutes. The centers will still be soft when they are removed from the oven but the cookies will be golden brown on top.

Makes 2½ to 3 dozen regular-sized cookies or 10 to 12 gargantuan cookies

Stocks

A good stock is the basis for a great soup or sauce. Homemade stocks will enhance the flavor of whatever you use them in. Cooking time varies. The darker and richer the flavor you need, the more cooking time necessary. But even a simple, quickly made Veggie Stock will make an average dish shine. Make one next time you are thinking of preparing a soup and bask in the fragrant, comforting scent of its simmer.

VEGGIE STOCK

This is a very basic vegetable stock. I like it to resemble a light chicken stock, so I peel the carrots and onions to eliminate any caramel color. I also don't strain the stock—I cut the vegetables nicely so I can use them later in a soup. The wine gives this stock an aromatic quality.

¼ cup olive oil
6 stalks celery
4 carrots, peeled
3 small onions, peeled
2 tablespoons dried thyme
3 bay leaves
½ teaspoon crushed red pepper flakes
2 garlic cloves, peeled and crushed
2 cups white wine

1. Pour olive oil into the bottom of a large stockpot. Cut celery, carrots, and onions into a ½-inch dice and place in stockpot.
2. Place stockpot over medium-high heat and cook vegetables until onions begin to turn translucent and carrots and celery soften. Add thyme, bay leaves, red pepper flakes, and garlic to the vegetables and cook for an additional minute so herbs can release their flavor. Add the white wine and bring to a simmer.
3. Once wine has reached a simmer, add enough water to cover the vegetables by 2 inches. Reduce the heat and continue to cook for 1 hour. Cool stock to room temperature before chilling. Stock will keep in the refrigerator for 5 to 7 days.

Makes 6 cups

ROASTED VEGGIE STOCK

Make sure the veggies are a rich mahogany color. The caramelizing is what gives this stock its flavor. Unlike regular Veggie Stock, Roasted Veggie Stock requires straining.

¼ cup olive oil
6 stalks celery
5 carrots
3 onions
2 apples
3 bay leaves
2 tablespoons dried thyme
2 garlic cloves, crushed
2 cups red wine

1. Preheat oven to 400°F. Pour oil into the bottom of a heavy roasting pan. Roughly chop celery and carrots into 1-inch pieces. Quarter onions and apples, leaving the skins on. Place the vegetables and apples in the roasting pan and sprinkle with bay leaves, thyme, and garlic. Bake for 1 hour. Give the vegetables a stir after 30 minutes to ensure even browning.
2. Check the vegetables after an hour. They should be mahogany in color; if not, return to the oven for another 30 minutes. Once they have reached the proper color, remove pan from the oven and place the vegetables in a large stockpot. Place the roasting pan over medium heat on top of the stove and whisk in the wine to deglaze the pan. Pour the juices and wine into the stockpot.
3. Place the stockpot over medium heat and add enough water to the pot to cover the vegetables by 2 inches. Simmer for 30 minutes. Remove from heat and strain. Discard the vegetables. Cool stock to room temperature before chilling. Stock will keep in the refrigerator for 5 to 7 days.

Makes 6 cups

CHICKEN STOCK

There is no substitute for a good chicken stock. It adds a rich, fragrant aroma and flavor to anything you make with it.

¼ cup olive oil
1 pound chicken backs
3 onions, quartered
3 carrots, cut into 1-inch pieces
4 stalks celery, cut into 1-inch pieces
1 tablespoon dried thyme
3 bay leaves
6 black peppercorns

1. Place oil in the bottom of a large, heavy-bottomed stockpot. Add the remaining ingredients and cook over medium heat until vegetables just begin to soften.
2. Cover vegetables and chicken with water and heat until mixture comes to a simmer. Reduce the heat and cover. Cook for 30 to 40 minutes. Remove from heat and strain. Discard the solids. Cool stock to room temperature before chilling. Stock will keep for 1 week in the refrigerator.

Makes about 10 cups

BROWN CHICKEN STOCK

This stock is rich enough in flavor to be used in place of veal or beef stock.

6 stalks celery
3 small onions
4 carrots
1 pound chicken backs
3 bay leaves
2 tablespoons dried thyme
2 garlic cloves, crushed
6 black peppercorns
2 cups red wine

1. Preheat oven to 400°F. Roughly chop celery, onions, and carrots into 1-inch pieces. Place all ingredients except wine in the bottom of a heavy roasting pan. Roast in the oven for 1 hour, stirring after 30 minutes to ensure even browning. When vegetables and chicken have an even mahogany color, remove pan from oven.
2. Transfer the vegetables and chicken to a large stockpot. Place the roasting pan over medium heat on top of the stove and add the red wine. Whisk, scraping up the brown bits, until pan is deglazed. Transfer the contents of the roasting pan to the stockpot.
3. Place the stockpot over medium heat and add enough water to cover the vegetables and bones. Simmer, uncovered, for 35 to 45 minutes. Remove from heat and strain, discarding the solids. Cool stock to room temperature before chilling. Stock will keep for 1 week in the refrigerator.

Makes about 10 cups

Sauces

When a beurre blanc is delicately draped over a beautiful portion of fresh grilled tuna, the sight alone can make your taste buds dance; the aroma will make them do the tango. Sauces do not have to be complicated to enhance a meal, just complementary to what you pair them with. All the recipes in this section are tried-and-true variations on such classic sauces as white sauce, aïoli, and beurre blanc. The trick is to turn a basic sauce recipe into your own by adding a favorite herb, spice, or flavoring. The right sauce will accentuate the meal, not overpower it, and beautify a dish, not disguise it. Use and enjoy the following recipes. They have served us well at the Biscuit, and I hope they will serve you well too.

RED SALSA

This roasted tomato salsa is spiked with chipotle peppers, which are smoked jalapeños. At the Biscuit we prefer to use the chipotles that are canned in adobo sauce.

1 pound ripe tomatoes
4 garlic cloves, minced
2 or 3 serrano peppers, stemmed (for a milder salsa, remove the seeds)
½ of a medium yellow onion, peeled
1 or 2 chipotle peppers in adobo sauce
1 teaspoon kosher salt
¼ cup chopped fresh cilantro

1. Preheat broiler.
2. Place the tomatoes, garlic, serranos, onion, and chipotles in a small roasting pan.
3. Broil, stirring frequently, until the vegetables are lightly charred.
4. Remove from the broiler and cool.
5. Place contents of roasting pan in a food processor or blender, add salt and cilantro, and puree until mixture reaches desired consistency. Chill until ready to serve.

Makes 3½ to 4 cups

GREEN SALSA

Tomatillos are a small, green variety of tomato that have a papery outer husk. If they are unavailable, you can use green tomatoes. To remove the husks easily, soak the tomatillos in water for a few minutes. It is easiest to peel them while they are still wet, so leave them in the water while you remove the husks. If you prefer a hotter salsa, leave the seeds in the serranos.

1 ½ pounds tomatillos
¼ cup minced yellow onion
2 garlic cloves, peeled
2 serrano peppers, stemmed and seeded
½ teaspoon kosher salt
¼ teaspoon white pepper
3 tablespoons chopped fresh cilantro

1. Preheat the oven to 350°F.
2. Peel the husks off the tomatillos. Place them in a roasting pan with the onion, garlic, and serrano peppers. Roast for 25 to 35 minutes. The tomatillos will break down and become juicy. Remove from oven and cool.
3. Place the roasted ingredients in a food processor and puree. Season with salt, white pepper, and cilantro. Chill until ready to serve.

Makes 2½ cups

BALSAMIC VINAIGRETTE

This is the recipe for our house dressing. Although it makes a lot of dressing, go ahead and whisk it up. You can use it in so many ways. We toss it with fresh, crisp field greens and serve it with almost every lunch and dinner entree. The dressing also makes a great marinade for grilled chicken. In fact, it's the secret ingredient for our popular warm chicken salad. Simply marinate chicken breasts in enough dressing to just cover them for at least 30 minutes in the refrigerator. Grill the chicken and serve warm on a bed of field greens that have been lightly tossed in the vinaigrette. To finish the salad, top with warm Rosemary Roasted Potatoes (page 40) and a liberal crumble of blue cheese. For a variation on this vinaigrette, add a few tablespoons of Basic Basil Pesto (page 107) or Roasted Red Pepper Mustard (page 103).

½ cup balsamic vinegar
½ cup Dijon mustard
1 ½ teaspoons freshly ground black pepper
1 ½ teaspoons kosher salt
3 garlic cloves, minced
1 ½ teaspoons dried oregano
1 ½ teaspoons dried basil
2 cups olive oil

1. Place vinegar, mustard, pepper, salt, garlic, oregano, and basil in a large mixing bowl and whisk together.
2. As you continue whisking, drizzle olive oil into the vinegar mixture in a slow, steady stream. Start slowly, then increase the speed very gradually to obtain a smooth emulsion. Vinaigrette can be refrigerated until ready to use. If the dressing separates, or breaks, bring it back to room temperature and whisk.

Makes 2 ½ cups

CREAMY HORSERADISH SAUCE

This spicy sauce works very well with our Turkey Meatloaf. Though horseradish on meatloaf may sound a little bizarre, give it a try. You will be amazed at how good they taste together.

2 tablespoons unsalted butter
2 tablespoons all-purpose flour
¾ cup heavy cream
1 cup milk
½ teaspoon kosher salt
¼ teaspoon white pepper
3 tablespoons grated horseradish

1. Place a medium-sized saucepan over medium-high heat and add butter. Once the butter has melted, whisk in flour. Remove from the heat and whisk in cream and milk, whisking in a slow, steady stream to prevent lumping.
2. Return the pan to the stove and cook over medium-high heat, stirring constantly, until the sauce thickens and becomes bubbly. Turn off the heat and stir in salt, white pepper, and horseradish. Serve warm, with Turkey Meatloaf (page 21) and Pudge (page 43).

Makes 2 cups

CHIPOTLE AÏOLI

Chipotles are smoked jalapeño peppers. They can be found in specialty stores and some super-markets and come dried or canned in adobo sauce. I prefer the canned version because the sauce gives a great flavor to almost any dish. Be careful. Chipotle peppers can be very hot. Make this sauce following the recipe the first time; if you discover you want it hotter, add a little more of the adobo sauce the next time. The heat from a chipotle can sneak up on you. At first everything seems okay, but give it a minute and it will burn at the back of your throat. It hurts so good, though.

3 or 4 chipotles in adobo sauce
1 tablespoon honey
1 tablespoon balsamic vinegar
1 tablespoon Dijon mustard
1 egg yolk
2 cups olive oil

1. Place chipotles, honey, vinegar, mustard, and egg yolk in a food processor or blender. Puree.
2. While machine is running, drizzle in olive oil in a slow, steady stream until aïoli thickens to the consistency of a thin mayonnaise. Serve sparingly with Black Bean Quesadillas (page 25). This sauce is also excellent with grilled fish or chicken. Be sure to refrigerate any leftovers.

Makes 2 ½ cups

ROASTED RED PEPPER MUSTARD

This mustard is a sweet, spicy condiment for meats, cheeses, and veggie burgers.

5 red peppers
²/₃ cup yellow mustard seeds
¹/₃ cup brown mustard seeds
1 cup dry mustard
1 tablespoon dried oregano
1 ½ cups brown sugar
1 cup white vinegar
½ cup beer

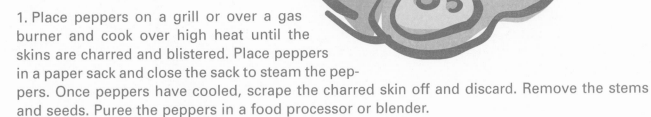

1. Place peppers on a grill or over a gas burner and cook over high heat until the skins are charred and blistered. Place peppers in a paper sack and close the sack to steam the peppers. Once peppers have cooled, scrape the charred skin off and discard. Remove the stems and seeds. Puree the peppers in a food processor or blender.

2. Combine peppers with remaining ingredients in a large, heavy-bottomed saucepan and place over medium heat. Bring mixture to a simmer, stirring frequently to prevent scorching. Cook for about 5 minutes. Mustard will thicken slightly. Remove from heat, cool, and refrigerate for 24 hours before using.

Makes about 4 cups

CRÈME FRAÎCHE

Crème fraîche is heavy cream that is thickened by the addition of a culture, usually buttermilk. The end result is a slightly tangy cream that can be used in a multitude of ways. You can stir it into fresh herbs and use it as a garnish on soups. You can use crème fraîche in place of sour cream in sauces, and it will not curdle when heated. You can also sweeten it and fold it into whipped cream for an excellent accompaniment to fresh berries.

2 cups heavy cream
2 tablespoons buttermilk

Place cream in a nonreactive container—glass is best. (A mason jar works great.) Stir in buttermilk. Cover and place in a warm (78°), dark spot for 24 hours. Stir after 24 hours. Mixture should be thick and creamy. If not, let sit out for another 8 hours and check again. Once mixture is the correct consistency, refrigerate until ready to use. It will keep for 1 week.

Makes 2½ cups

CILANTRO CRÈME FRAÎCHE
Add 2 tablespoons of finely minced cilantro to the Crème Fraîche.

TOMATO COULIS

A light, fragrant tomato sauce is invaluable. Use it as a dip for bruschetta or as a quick pasta sauce. Grill chicken or fish and serve this sauce as a dip. Tomato Coulis is also great with eggs, polenta, and Italian sausage.

2 tablespoons olive oil
2 garlic cloves, minced
¼ cup packed fresh basil leaves
½ of a small onion, thinly sliced crosswise
1 (28 ounce) can whole Roma tomatoes with their juice
¼ cup balsamic vinegar
½ teaspoon kosher salt
½ teaspoon freshly ground black pepper

1. Place a large, heavy-bottomed saucepan over medium-high heat. Add olive oil. When the olive oil is hot and almost smoking, add garlic and basil. (Heating the oil to almost smoking before adding basil seals in the color and flavor of the herb.)
2. When the garlic is lightly browned, add onion and cook until it just begins to turn translucent. Add the tomatoes. Stir in balsamic vinegar, salt, and pepper and simmer for 15 minutes. Remove from heat and puree in a blender or food processor. Serve hot.

Makes 3½ cups

JUST A BASIC BEURRE BLANC

A good butter sauce is hard to beat, and unexpectedly easy to make. It can be seasoned with just about anything from fresh herbs or chipotles to tamari and ginger. Use only the best butter available; lesser butters have water added to them, which can cause the sauce to separate, or break. European-style butters such as Plugra are homogenized with much less water. If your sauce does break, don't panic. Remove it from the heat and place a few tablespoons of cream in the bottom of a clean saucepan. Bring cream to a simmer and gradually whisk in the offending sauce.

½ cup white wine
1 tablespoon minced shallots
½ cup heavy cream
2 sticks (1 cup) unsalted butter, cut into tablespoons,
  at room temperature
¼ teaspoon kosher salt
¼ teaspoon white pepper

OPTIONAL FLAVORS TO ADD TO THE REDUCTION*
1 tablespoon tamari
Zest and juice of 1 lemon
Zest and juice of 1 orange
1 tablespoon of your favorite chopped fresh herb
1 chipotle pepper
1 to 1 ½ tablespoons fresh raspberries

* Let your imagination be your guide, but be careful adding anything that may have oil in it, such as pesto, because the sauce will become more delicate and likely to separate.

1. Place a small, heavy-bottomed saucepan over medium heat. Add wine, shallots, and any optional flavor to the pan and simmer until mixture is reduced by two-thirds. (There should be very little liquid left in the pan.)
2. Add cream and reduce by two-thirds again. Reduce the heat and gradually whisk in butter, a tablespoon at a time. As each tablespoon begins to melt, add the next. Mixture should barely be simmering on the edges of the pan while you are adding the butter. When all the butter has been added, remove pan from the heat and stir in salt and pepper. Keep warm until ready to serve.

Makes 1½ cups

BASIC BASIL PESTO

I am including this recipe because I believe that a good jar of pesto is an invaluable tool in a kitchen. It can be made, stored, and frozen for emergencies. Toss some pesto with pasta and you have a quick and easy meal. Add it to vinaigrettes or marinades for a boost in flavor. I prefer to use extra-virgin olive oil with pesto. Since you don't cook the oil, the essential flavors of the extra-virgin oil are not lost and merge together wonderfully with the other pesto ingredients. Pine nuts are traditionally used to make pesto, but if they are not available, walnuts will work just as well.

2 cups packed fresh basil leaves
½ cup toasted pine nuts
4 garlic cloves, minced
½ cup grated high-quality Parmesan cheese, preferably Parmigiano-Reggiano
½ teaspoon kosher salt
½ teaspoon freshly ground black pepper
⅔ cup extra-virgin olive oil

1. Place basil, pine nuts, garlic, cheese, salt, and pepper in a food processor or blender. Puree.
2. While machine is running, gradually add oil to make a paste. If you are not using the pesto right away, place in a container and cover the entire surface of the pesto with a thin coat of olive oil to prevent discoloring. Pesto will keep in the refrigerator for several weeks, and it freezes very well for up to 2 months.

Makes 2 cups

Sweet Accompaniments

The right garnish on a dessert plate can turn an ordinary brownie into something extraordinary. Drizzling some Razzberry Sauce and Extra-Rich Chocolate Sauce over that little square of chocolate cake makes it seem truly special. This is the kind of extra touch we try to do often at the Flying Biscuit. By placing a container of homemade Cranberry Apple Butter on the table for people to enjoy with their Flying Biscuit or Organic Oatmeal Pancake, we give everyone an added made-from-scratch flavor to their food. The following recipes turn a good dessert, pancake, or French toast dish into a memorable meal.

CRANBERRY APPLE BUTTER

Cranberry Apple Butter is a staple at the Biscuit. We make huge batches of the stuff. One batch is about 7 ½ gallons, and we make a batch three times a week. That is a lot of apple butter. It is hard to beat a biscuit hot out of the oven topped with Cranberry Apple Butter.

2 cups dark brown sugar
1 cinnamon stick
1 ¼ teaspoons ground cinnamon
1 teaspoon ground nutmeg
1 teaspoon ground cloves
1 cup freshly squeezed orange juice
2 cups cranberries
10 Granny Smith apples, peeled, cored, and thinly sliced

1. Place sugar, spices, and orange juice in a large, heavy-bottomed saucepan. Bring to a simmer and add the cranberries. Cook over medium heat until cranberries begin to pop.
2. Add the apples and cook over low heat, stirring frequently. Cook until apples are tender and falling apart. Puree contents of saucepan in a food processor or mash with a potato masher until smooth and thick. Cool and serve with hot biscuits. Cranberry Apple Butter will keep for 2 to 3 weeks in the refrigerator.

Makes 4½ cups

STRAWBERRY RHUBARB JAM

In the summer, when apples and cranberries are not at their peak, this jam makes a good alternative at the restaurant to our ever-popular Cranberry Apple Butter.

1 quart fresh strawberries
1 pound fresh rhubarb
3 cups sugar
2 tablespoons lemon juice
1 ½ teaspoons quick tapioca

1. Clean and hull strawberries and slice in half. Clean rhubarb and slice into ½-inch pieces.
2. Place strawberries, rhubarb, sugar, and lemon juice in a large, heavy-bottomed saucepan. Let sit for 15 minutes. Add tapioca and let sit another 15 minutes. Bring mixture to a simmer and cook for 45 minutes to an hour at a very low simmer. To test for doneness, place a tablespoon of jam on a plate and refrigerate for a few minutes. When you take it out of the refrigerator, the jam should just begin to skin over and have the consistency of jelly. If jam has not reached the desired consistency, continue to cook, checking for doneness every 20 minutes. Cool and refrigerate. Jam will keep for 2 to 3 weeks.

Makes 2 ½ quarts

FRESH BERRY COMPOTE

Make this during the summer, when all the berries are at their peak.

1 pint strawberries
1 pint blueberries
½ pint blackberries
½ pint raspberries
1 vanilla bean, or ½ teaspoon vanilla extract
¾ cup water
½ cup sugar

1. Clean and hull strawberries, slice in half, and place in a large bowl. Rinse blueberries and remove any debris. Add to the strawberries. Gently pick through the blackberries and raspberries and add to the bowl.
2. Split the vanilla bean in half lengthwise and carefully scrape out the seeds. Place seeds and bean (or vanilla extract) in a small saucepan, along with water and sugar. Bring to a simmer over medium heat and cook until sugar is dissolved. Pour syrup over berries and cool. Remove the vanilla bean before serving. (The used vanilla bean can be rinsed, patted dry, and placed in a sugar bowl. It will make the sugar very aromatic.) Compote will keep for 2 to 3 days in the refrigerator.

Makes 3 cups

RAZZBERRY SAUCE

This is an all-purpose dessert sauce, excellent with anything chocolate, or served with your favorite pancakes or French toast.

2 cups fresh or frozen raspberries
½ cup sugar
¼ cup water

Place berries, sugar, and water in a small saucepan. Bring to a simmer over medium heat. Cook until the berries break down and the sauce begins to thicken. Remove from heat, cool, and puree in a blender or food processor. Serve at room temperature.

Makes 2 cups

KAHLUA ANGLAISE

Anglaise is a very trendy dessert sauce. This one is flavored with Kahlua, but if you have another favorite liqueur, give it a try.

4 large egg yolks
½ cup sugar
2 cups heavy cream
2 tablespoons Kahlua

1. Whisk together egg yolks and sugar in a small bowl until light in color and smooth. Place cream in a small saucepan and bring to a simmer over medium heat. Remove from heat.
2. Whisk ½ cup of the hot cream into egg yolk-sugar mixture. Whisk yolks and cream back into remaining cream in the saucepan and return to the heat. Cook, stirring continuously with a wooden spoon, until cream coats the back of the spoon. Remove from stove and stir in Kahlua. Chill until ready to serve. Serve cold.

Makes 2½ cups

EXTRA-RICH CHOCOLATE SAUCE

My criteria for a good chocolate sauce are that it is easy to make and tastes great. This recipe meets these goals. Serve this sauce warm over ice cream, or use it to garnish a dessert plate. It is thick, rich, and bittersweet.

1 ½ cups half and half
1 cup confectioners' sugar
¼ cup cocoa powder
8 ounces semisweet chocolate, finely chopped
4 tablespoons unsalted butter
1 teaspoon vanilla extract

1. Place half and half, confectioners' sugar, cocoa powder, and semisweet chocolate in the top of a double boiler. Place over a pot of barely simmering water and cook, stirring frequently, for 15 to 20 minutes.
2. Remove the double boiler from the heat and whisk in the butter, a tablespoon at a time. When the butter has blended into the sauce, whisk in the vanilla. Serve warm off the stove. Refrigerate any leftovers. Sauce can be reheated over a double boiler.

Makes 2 ½ cups

INDEX

INDEX

INDEX

INDEX

INDEX

INDEX

April Moon has been the chef at the Flying Biscuit Cafe since the restaurant opened in 1993. Before coming to the Biscuit, April was a chef at Partner's, one of Atlanta's premier restaurants, and worked at the Ocean City Diner in San Francisco. She studied culinary arts at the Asheville Buncomb Technical College and at the Culinary Institute of America. She lives in Stone Mountain, Georgia, with her husband, David Harper, and their two daughters, Hanna and Emma.